Māṇikkavāsakar's Mystic Poem

Sivapurāṇam

English Rendering, Meanings, & Pan-Cultural Reflections

V. V. Raman

Create Space

CONTENTS

Manikkavasakar's heart-melting strains are full of living faith and devotion, and every little poem of the author exhibits his longing that "He must make him His."

- **M. S. Purnalingam Pillai**

Preface

Fifty years ago (in 1962) my father, (the late) Pudukkōṭṭai Sundaram Varadaraja Aiyar, published a slender volume in Tamil, entitled *Chiva purāṇa chirpam*. It was published by Pudukkottai Prapañcha Joti Printing Service. The first sentence in the book's introduction was "The imperishable wealth of a people is contained in their arts and literature." My father had instilled this idea in me since my boyhood days.

He initiated me into Vedic chants, making me learn by rote Purusha Sūktam, Rudram, and more, He developed in me love for the Tamil language and (classical) Tamil literature. I studied Tirukkuraḷ and Kamba Rāmāyaṇam under my father, but it was only through his book of 1962 that I came to know about and read Sivapurāṇam.

My father also fostered in me a sensitivity for matters religious and spiritual in a deeper sense. I recall reading with him Sivavākkiyar's lines:

What are temples, tell me!
And what are sacred tanks?
O you poor slaves who worship
in temples and tanks!
Temples are in the mind.

Tanks are in the mind.
There is no Becoming,
There is no Unbecoming,
None, none whatever!

He also instigated in me a fondness for (classical) English literature which I extended to the literature of a few other languages also. I have relished this all my life.

Most of all, my father taught me to respect all faith systems of the human family. This was quite natural for many Hindus at one time. He also warned me against cultural chauvinism. Now the world has changed in many ways, but, on these matters, I have not.

Over the years I have been reading and reflecting on the mystical poetry of Sivapurāṇam. Last year it occurred to me that perhaps I should post my reflections on the internet. This book is the result of those efforts.

I am grateful to Tiru Pathmarajah Nagalingam, a Tamil scholar and devotee of Lord Shiva, for making valuable comments on the manuscript prior to publication, and for writing a Foreword for this book. I would also like to thank Dr. Kumar for his suggestions. I appreciate the others who made the brief statements that you read on the back cover.

MANIKKAVASAKAR'S SIVAPURANAM

I have no idea how many modern English-educated Tamils, let alone Hindus, read Māṇikkavāsakar's Sivapurāṇam. I suspect that few beyond the Saiva Siddhāntam community of the Tamil world (except for some foreign scholars in the field) have even heard of this work. It is my hope that this book will stir their interest in this gem in the treasure chest of Tamil religious poetry.

I take full responsibility for any errors that might have crept into my work, and for my sometimes unorthodox commentaries. It was all done with reverance for the poet, respect for the culture, and love for the grander aspects of tradition.

I dedicate this book to my parents: Varadaraja Aiyar and Lakshmi Ammal who showed me the way.

V. V. Raman

Ames, IA

February 20, 2012

Foreword

திருச்சிற்றம்பலம்

Tiruchitrambalam

The Sivapurāṇam is the first hymn of the 51 hymn Tiruvāsakam, a volume of Tamil hymns composed in the ninth century by the Saiva bhakti poet Māṇikkavāsakar in Tiruperunturai, Tamil Nadu. It is considered to be the first of the saint's hymns and constitutes the eighth volume of the Tirumuṟai, the sacred anthology of Saiva Siddhānta. The sacred mystic poetry glorifies God Siva in metered verses and reveals the character, aspirations and culture of the Tamil people. Among the finest of Hindu shastras, the Sivapurāṇam deals with the fundamental principles of Hinduism and is a complete shastra by itself.

A famous Tamil saying is, "those who do not melt for Thiruvasagam will never melt for any other."

A nineteenth century English translator of the work George U. Pope declared that, "The hymns are recited daily in all the great Saiva temples of South India, are on every one's lips and are as dear to the vast multitudes of excellent people there, as the Psalms of David are to Jews and Christians."

Kamil Zvelebil, an eminent modern scholar of the Tamil language and literature wrote: "In Tamil Culture the works of art and literature are among the most remarkable contributions of the Tamil creative genius to the world's cultural treasure and should be familiar to the whole world and admired and beloved by all in the same way as the poems of Homer, the dramas of Shakespeare, the pictures of Rembrandt, the cathedrals of France and the sculptures of Greece .... The school of Bhakti .... Saiva, which is one of those most sincere and passionate efforts of man to grasp the Absolute, and its supreme literary expression in the works of Manickvasagar.." (*Tamil Contribution to World Civilisation* -Vol. V, No. 4. October, 1956).

I have been chanting this hymn for 40 years now and yet there is so much more meaning to it that I discovered after reading these commentaries. In capsulised form it contains some of the basic precepts of the Saiva Siddhānta philosophy. I have read a variety and number of Sanskrit and Tamil hymns including Tulsidas, and if I am asked which is the single greatest hymn in all of Hindu scriptures, I would say it is the Sivapurāṇam, followed by the Sri Rudram of the Yajur Veda. The Sivapurāṇam is the Michelangelo of Tamil hymns.

Dr. V.V. Raman, the recipient of the Raja Rao Award (2006), is a multifaceted personality. He is a philosopher, physicist, writer, and author of original works. Deeply versed in India's culture and religion, he has written on the historical, social, and philosophical aspects of physics/science, as well as on India's heritage. He has authored several books including *Scientific Perspectives, Glimpses of Ancient Science and Scientists, Variety in Religion and Science, and Variety in Science History*. He has been hailed as an Acharya, Religious Teacher, by Navyashastra, a Hindu organization in the United States.

Having known Dr. Raman through his earlier writings and reviewing this work where he compares Māṇikkavāsakar's spiritual outpourings with other philosophical systems, poets, thinkers and western literature, I have no hesitation in saying he is one of the greatest living Hindu scholars, at home in Tamil, Sanskrit and a dozen other languages.

The book is an invaluable contribution to Shaivism, Hinduism and to the English speaking world. I would place this book at the forefront of all books on Hinduism in English. Spiritual awakenings are among the most worth searching in life. In this book we have one such quest.

திருச்சிற்றம்பலம்

Tiruchitrambalam.

Pathmarajah Nagalingam: Hindu writer, teacher, activist.

www.siddha.com.myKuala Lumpur, 26th January 2012

Thanaletchmy

thanaletchmygengadoran@gmail.com

omnamasivaya

INTRODUCTION

A Brief Note on Saiva Religion

It is said that Saivam (the worship of Lord Shiva) is one of six major religious traditions in South India. They are collectively referred to as *Āruvakai Samayam*. We may call them the Tamil *Shad-dharma* in Sanskrit or *Hexaltry* (Worship of the Six). In this religious tradition one worships one of six different Divinities: the Sun, Lord Gaṇapati, Lord Murugan, Shakti, Vishṇu, and Shiva. Each of these schools bears a different name: Sauram, Gaṇapatyam, Kaumaram, Vaishṇavam, Sakhtam, and Saivam.

Some Tamil followers of Saivam prefer not to be called Hindus. It is, however, difficult to separate out the philosophical worldview of Saiva Siddhāntam from the core principle of the culturally unifying tradition of Indic vintage that the world recognizes as Hinduism.

Saiva Siddhāntam

Saiva Siddhāntam is an ancient Indic religious-spiritual tradition. It is based on philosophical insights, doctrinal positions, and sublime poetry. It takes Lord Shiva (also spelt as Siva) as the fundamental undergirding principle in the Cosmos. It has a North Indian as well as a South Indian version. In both systems abstract Siva is transcendent as well as immanent, but it also has a personal form. Divinity is beyond categories. Those who worship it in the Shiva mode are beyond the constraints of caste and creed, they are supposed to see Divinity in one and all.

Saiva Siddhāntam attributes sacredness to all life. It believes that the Divine gives grace to all who seek it, sometimes even to those who do not. All life may be regarded as an expression of grace. The Divine participates in the course of every life, yet remains untouched by it all. All of creation is nothing but a reflection of divine ecstasy.

Three entities are regarded real: *pati* which is the Divine, *pasu* which is the soul, and *pāsam* which is the rope that binds the *pasu* to the worldly domain and constrains it from receiving the light from *pati*. Through *jñāna* and *bhakti*, the bonds of *pāsam* may be cut, thus enabling one to attain ultimate freedom. Some modern scholars have given slightly different interpretations of these three key elements of the system, but they need not concern us here, because this is not a treatise on the subject.

Another important idea in the framework of

Saiva Siddhāntam is that for interaction between the Divine and the human to occur, both should be on the same plane. Either the Divine comes down to our level (*avatāra*), or we must raise ourselves to the level of the Divine. This transformation is said to occur in two stages: first there is the nullification of the physical dimension, or rather purification of the gross elements of which the body is formed (*bhūtashuddhi*), and then through mantras the body becomes one of spiritual energy (*shaktadeha*). By this process of *sivakaraṇa* (transformation into Siva), enlightenment is achieved.

In the Tamil tradition there are fourteen canonical texts expounding the principles of Saiva Siddhānta. Of these *Sivajñānabōdam* of Maikaṇḍa Dēvar is regarded as the most important. Attention has been drawn by scholars like Dr. Loganathan of Malaysia to facets of inner astronomy (*kuṇḍali* based depth psychology), the political philosophy of human freedom, Existentialism, and so forth.

Aside from their metaphysical and spiritual visions, the Saiva poets of the tradition have made some of the most outstanding contributions to Tamil poetry. The Saiva hymns are more than *bhakti*-poetry. Their hymns initiate new kinds of philosophical thinking. Some of these were developed in the later Meykaṇḍa Shāstras Their songs of these poets are moving, and their visions penetrating. These poets are remembered and their works recited in Shiva temples all over the Tamil world. They are venerated as few poets are in any culture.

The Sivapurāṇam of Māṇikkavāsakar is pure devotional poetry. Its beauty lies in the Tamil in which it is composed and chanted in Shiva temples of the Tamil world. Its aesthetic appeal and spiritual potency are considerably diminished in any translation. But one can still appreciate its content even in another language. The Tamil Sivapurāṇam is not to be confused with the Shiva Purāna of Sanskrit literature.

Māṇikkavāsakar

Māṇikkavāsakar (9th century?) is one of the foremost poets in the history of Tamil literature. He is revered as a saint in Tamil Shai-vism. Much of what we know about this bright star in the firmament of Tamil poetry is from two sources: the *Tiruvādavūr Purāṇam* and *Tiruviḷaiyāḍāl Purāṇam*.

Vāḍavūrār (Man from Vāḍavūr) composed devotional songs at a tender age. His reputation drew the attention of the Paṇḍya king Saundara of

Madurai. He was appointed prime minister when still quite young.

It is said that Vaḍavūrār was sent by the king on a mission to buy horses from a neighboring realm. On the way, he was distracted by a sage who, it is said, was Shiva himself in human form. Inspired by the instructions of this charismatic sage, the poet spent the king's cash to build a Shiva temple. This infuriated the king, and the religiously inspired minister was imprisoned and tortured. The saintly poet is believed to have gotten out of his cell miraculously. And he began to compose and sing hymns to Shiva. Words flowed from his lips like sparkling gems. This won him the epithet of Māṇikkavāsakar: one who utters ruby-like words.

Māṇikkavāsakar's *Tiruvāsakam* contains some of the finest poems of the Tamil bhakti mode. It begins with Sivapurāṇam. It is difficult for the lay reader to fully appreciate the depth of feeling and spiritual yearning in *Tiruvāsakam.* Spiritual poetry of this kind is an outpouring of the heart, and addressed to the Unfathomable Mystery. Sometimes it seems to wander in the wilderness like the reckless coloring on canvas by a master of the abstract school of painting. When people read the work, some resonate with awe, others are bewildered, yet others turn away.

Māṇikkavāsakar also wrote another book, called *Tirukkōvaiyār* which is a work on love: from romantic love at first sight to marital love and love with prostitutes. It is intriguing that the saint composed a work of this genre. Commentators have explained this by suggesting that the work is an allegory of the soul in quest of Shiva. Even with this interpretation, it is not among the poet's works that are recited in temples.

Māṇikkavāsakar did much to revert the Tamil world from Jaina and Buddhist influences. Like other poets of that Hindu revival phase in the South, he is said to have been harsh towards their doctrines.

It is said that sometimes Māṇikkavāsakar went through periods of spiritual delirium during which he lost himself in a heightened level of god-intoxication. Sometimes he went through deep depression when he felt that Shiva was not within reach. We are reminded of similar experience es that Saint Ramakrishna and other saints had. After a series of such alternating phases, the author of Sivapurāṇam is said to have attained full liberation in the holy center at Chidambaram. Here his name has been deservedly immortalized. The glory of

India's spiritual tradition shines in the poetry and psalms of her sage-poets.

A note on Tiruchitrambalam

Within the precincts of the famed tample of Naṭarāja in the holy city of Chidambaram there is a little sacred spot known as Tiruchitrambalam. Here, for ages the Tiruvāsakam has been read and recited with the appropriate canonical decorum.

In the Saiva spiritual tradition, any reading or recital of a sacred work of Saiva Siddhānta should begin and end with invocation of Tiruchitrambalam.

In this day and age when unholy alliances between religion and politics are as rampant as untenable mixing of religion and science, there have been some problems with the recital of *Tiruvāsakam* in Tiruchitrambalam. According to a news item a few years ago, some of the Sanskritist managers of the Naṭarāja Temple banned the chanting of this Tamil scripture, declaring that only Sanskrit mantras were permitted there, as if to show the world that theological bigotry is not the prerogative of any particular religious group or subgroup. More seriously, it is a symptom of the grave spiritual crisis in the Hindu world, prompted by both internal and external forces.

On Mystical poetry

The conviction or the awareness of a dimension of reality that transcends space and time has been part of human culture since time immemorial. A good many human beings have claimed they have recognized and realized that dimension. But that dimension seems to defy efforts by logic and science to put it into evidence or to prove its non-existence.

Some who have had the experience or only a glimpse of that which which is beyond sensorily tractable aspects of the world have articulated it in poetic modes. These are the mystic poets. Like music and humor, every culture and language has its own mystic poets. The sufi poets of the Islamic tradition (like Rumi and Hafiz), the Saint poets of the Christian tradition (like St. Francis of Asissi and St. Teresa Avila), the Vaishṇava poets of the Hindu tradition (like Sri Chaitanya and Meera Bai), and some English poets (like William Blake and Samuel Coleridge) come to mind. But there are many more of them in these and in other traditions. Māṇikkavāsakar belongs to that prestigious ga-laxy of mystic poets.

Though mystic poets have often spoken in terms of the deistic images of their own tradition, there have also been many who go be-yond the cultural confines within which they grew. Thus, for example the Tamil poet Sivavā- kkiyar wrote:

He is not Hari, He is not the Lord Siva.
He is the Ultimate Cause,
In the Beyond of the Beyond,
Transcending Blackness, Redness, and Whiteness,
Immoveable.
Try to understand:
He is not big, He is not small.
He is Infinite Distance, Immovable,
Transcending even Supreme Quiessence.

St. Teresa Avila said:

Let nothing upset you, let nothing startle you.
All things pass; God does not change.
Patience wins all it seeks.
Whoever has God lacks nothing:
God alone is enough.

The mystic poet Bhakta Kabir sang thus:

The bhakti path winds in a delicate way.
On this path there is no asking and no not asking.
The ego simply disappears the moment you touch him.
The joy of looking for him is so immense
Tthat you just dive in, and coast around

like a fish in the water.
If anyone needs a head, the lover leaps up to offer his.

St. Francis of Asissi was another mystic poet. Here are some lines from his Canticle of Brother Sun, reminding us of the Gāyatri mantra

Most High, all-powerful, all-good Lord,
All praise is Yours, all glory, all honour and all blessings.
To you alone, Most High, do they belong, and no mortal lips are worthy to pronounce Your Name.
Praised be You my Lord with all Your creatures, especially Sir Brother Sun,
Who is the day through whom You give us light.
And he is beautiful and radiant with great splendour,
Of You Most High, he bears the likeness.
Praised be You, my Lord, through Sister Moon and the stars,
In the heavens you have made them bright, precious and fair.

And from William Blake:
And all must love the human form,

In heathen, turk, or jew;
Where Mercy, Love, & Pity dwell
There God is dwelling too.

Mystic poets are not mere versifiers. They utter from the depths of their hearts the sublime experiences they have had, not through reading or reflection, but by listening to an inner voice that others cannot hear. Their poetry is like the report of a traveler to a distant land, a realm that is beyond our reach. The poet William Blake said: "The man who never in his mind and thoughts travel'd to heaven is no artist." The statement is equally true if we replace the word artist by mystic poet.

Māṇikkavāsakar paid homage to Lord Shiva in many sacred temples, and finally reached the great temple of Naṭarāja in Chidambaram where, it is said, his manuscript bore the seal of Lord Shiva Himself. No matter who he was, where he lived or when, we celebrate that great soul who has left for generations to come this work we read and reflect upon upon his work to this day.

The recurring themes in this work are the following: deep devotion and ardent love for the Shiva Principle, both its abstract and personified aspects; gratitude and humility in the cointext of the grace received; Shiva as the power that can release one from re-birth, and pleas for the same; the karma framework. All this will be repeated several times in the framework of Saiva Sid- dhāntam. Why the repetition? Because that is how one speaks to the beloved: one never tires of declaring one's love again and again.

My goal in this book is not to speak on behalf of any particular religion or philosophy. Many have done this eloquently and effectively. What I will be doing is to reflect on one of the great examples of mystical poetry. In every line of this work the sensitive reader can feel the the poet's immersion in the Shiva Principle. He expresses his involvement with the Divine with uncommon devotion, love, and faith. Whether one is a Shaiva, Vaishṇava, or Hindu, whether or not one is a Tamil, one can still read, admire, and reflect on Māṇikkavasar's immortal poem.

Approximate Pronunciation guide

ā (ஆ)	*aa* as in f*a*r (f*aa*r)	
d (த)	as *th* in *th*is.	
ḍ (ட)	as *d* in *d*og	
ē (ஏ)	as *ay* in d*ay*	
ī (ஈ)	as *ee*	in b*ee*
ḷ (ள)	as *l*	in p*l*um (closest)
ṇ (ண)	as *n*	in mo*n*ey (cloest)
ṅ (ங)	as *ng*	in so*ng*.
ñ (ஞ)	as *ny*	in So*ny*a.
ō (ஓ)	as *oa*	in b*oa*t.
ṟ (ற)	as rr	in purr.
t (த)	as *th*	in *th*ink (closest)
ṭ (ட)	as *t*	in *t*op
u	as u	in p*u*t
ū (ஊ)	as *oo*	in f*oo*l
z (ழ)	as su	in mea*s*ure (closest)

Lines of the Chant
Word Meanings
Explanatory Reflections

1.1

நமச்சிவாய வாழ்க
நாதன்
தாள் வாழ்க

namachchivāya vāzga
nādaan tāl vāzga!
May Siva's name endure!
May the feet of the Lord
(who guides me) endure!

Word meanings

namah - respectful bowing, veneration. Here, name

sivāya - to, of, Siva

vāzga - May (it, He) live for ever in auspiciousness!

nāthan - (of) the Lord

tāḷ - feet

vāzga - May (they) live for ever in auspiciousness!

Explanatory reflections

In the Shaiva tradition, the combination of these five (Tamil) letters *na-ma-si-vā-ya* form the most sacred mantra: a chant that has esoteric significance. So it is known as *tiruvaindezuttu*: (*tiru aindu ezhuttu*) sacred five-letter. It is believed that if this mantra is appropriately received from a guru, and one chants it on a regular basis, that would be a means of attaining spiritual fulfillment.

Each of the constituent letters has a hidden meaning. The letter *na* represents occult power of *nādan*: the Lord; *ma* represents water or the world; *si* is for *sivam; vā* is that which welcomes us; *ya* is said to stand for the embodied soul (*yākkai* means body). All the truths of the entire Sivapurāṇam are said to be enshrined in this *pañcākshara* (pentasyllabic) mantra.

Volumes have been written on the esoteric significance of the *pañcākshara.* The five syllables represent Siva's five faces, the five elements, etc. In this context, it simply means, *I bow down to Lord Siva.* Some have suggested that it is more appropriate to interpret the mantra as *nāmasivāya*: the name of Siva, because we pray for its enduring persistence. None of us can fathom Divine Wholeness. So we refer to it by a name. It is through that name that we connect with infinity. When we pray for the enduring of that name, we are praying that our own connection with the eternal principle may endure.

We are known by our names. But the names we bear are associated with our bodies in the present birth. In another incarnation, we will have a different name. But the Lord's name lives for ever. It says in the Ecclesiastics: "A good name endureth for ever." So we speak of the immortal permanence of the name of Shiva, the enduring Cosmic Principle.

The importance of attaching sanctity to God's name is not unique to the Saiva tradition. Vaishṇavas have their twelve-syllabic mantra, *aum namo bhagavatē vāsudevāya*. In Buddhism one has, *oṃ maṇi padme huṃ.* The name of God is sacred in all religious traditions. Whether as Yaweh or as Allah, it should not be taken in vain. As it says in the Old Testament, "The name of the Lord is a strong power." Likewise, the Lord's prayer in the Christian tradition begins with the lines:

Pater noster quia in coelis
Sanctificatur nomen tuum.
Our Father Who art in Heaven
Hallowed by Thy Name.

The word *vāzga!* means: May (someone, something) live for ever in auspiciousness. It will be used several times. It is more than the French *Vive!* or the Italian *Viva!* which simply mean: May (something or someone) live long ! The word *vāzka!* is also said to reflect the bliss of the one who chants the mantra.

In the first part of the first line of Sivapurāṇam,

the word *vāzga* has been split into two syllables: *vā āzka,* in order to maintain the prosodic meter.

We do not know by what mystery we were brought to the recognition of the Divine. That which guided us to this cosmic consciousness is the Lord's grace. In the poetic vision of Hindu spirituality, and from this, in Indic tradition, one attains spiritual fulfillment by expressing one's reverence to the feet of God (or of parents, teachers, elders). So it says that we pay homage to the feet of *nādan* (the Lord).

We may note that the mantra *namah sivāya* is not in the Rig Veda but in the *Rudrastadhyayi* which is part of the Yajur Veda. Thus, this mantra of the Tamil *Saiva Siddhāntam* tradition has Vedic links. The name Siva has many meanings. Commonly it is taken to signify auspiciousness. In the Tamil tradition, aside from being an appellation for Lord Siva, some of the other meanings of the word *sivam* are bliss, heaven, and supreme deity.

1.2

இமைப்பொழுதும் என் நெஞ்சில் நீங்காதான் தாள் வாழ்க

imaippozudum enneñjil

nīṅgādān tāḷ vāzga!

Who will not move away from my heart

even for a moment, may His feet endure!

Word meanings

imai - blinking of an eye;

pozutum - even for the time;

imaippozutum - not even for a moment

en - my;

neñjil - from (the) heart;

nīṅgādān - who will not move away from;

tāḷ - feet;

vāzga - May (they) live for ever in auspiciousness!

Explanatory Reflections

It is easy to repeat the aphorism, *tat tvam asi*: Thou art That. The significance of the phrase is that the divine principle is within each one of us. But how many of us truly feel this deep in our hearts? If we did, our behavior and reactions to people and events would be very different. It is true that when we are in a place of worship, when we pray, and when we are entertaining pious thoughts, we are never tempted to do anything harmful or hurtful.

Rather, we show kindness and love, and are helpful to others. But outside of that context and in the face of unkind, unpleasant, and hurting people, it is difficult to imagine they are also sparks of the divine, and act accordingly.

This line suggests that if we wish to lead a life of goodness, love and helpfulness, we must be conscious of the God's presence in our hearts. Conversely, as long as that awareness is in us, life will be fulfilling. So the poet pays homage to the Lord Who will not be away from his heart even for a fleeting moment. Then again, cherishing God in one's heart constantly is also a mark of intense and unfailing love, for the one we love is always present in the heart, and we will never allow that which is dear to us to move away from our heart. Our poet says that when we are in God's grace, every moment is worth a whole life. Recall Goethe's line: *Die Gegenwart ist eine mächtige Gottin*: The present is a powerful deity. If God is present in that present, that is truly a powerful moment. Or again, Friedrich Schiller wrote, "What one refuses in a minute no eternity will return." Our poet says in a more positive way that if we accept the Divine at every moment, we will be part of eternity.

The phrase *kaṇṇimaippozhutu* means the time it

takes for twinkling of the eye, i.e. an instant. The German word for an instant is *Augenblick*: the blink of the eye.

1.3

கோகழி ஆண்ட குருமணிதன் தாள் வாழ்க

kōkazi āṇḍān kurumaṇi-tan tāḷvāzga!

May the feet of the spotless gem of Kōkazi endure for ever!

Word meanings

Kōkazi - name of a holy place in Tami Nadu.

āṇḍān - who ruled.

kurumaṇi-tan - of spotless gem

tāḷ - feet

vāzga - May (they) live for ever in auspiciousness

Explanatory reflections

Kōkazi may be taken as a reference to the holy city of Tiruvāvaḍuturai. The allusion is to the grace that devotees received at the temples in these places. Tiruvāvaḍuturai has the shrine of Lord Siva as Māsilamanīsar (māsu-ila-maṇi-īsar: Spot-less-gem-Lord). The hymns of *Tēvā-ram* sing the praise of more than 275 Shiva temples. The gem is also known as *kurumaṇi*. According to sacred history, Pārvati once assumed the form of a cow and worshiped Siva here. This is a place of pilgrimage where there is a fig tree (Ficus religiosa, *arasamaram*) under which, as per tradition, the poet Tirumūlar composed the Tirumantiram. It was here that another Tamil sage-poet of the Saiva tradition, Sambandar, is said to have received his grace from Lord Siva. Siva manifested Himself as Tyāgarājar here. To commemorate this, there is an annual festival here known as Tyāgarāja-Sundara-Naḍanam. Some scholars have suggested that the reference is to Tiruppenduṟai.

The word *kō* also means cow (*pasu*). In Saiva Siddhānta, it is a metaphor for the soul. Likewise, *kazi* meaning ocean, is a metaphor for human life. The idea is that the Lord enables the soul to cross the ocean of human existence. This is a frequent imagery in Hindu theology. The journey of life is wrought with turbulence and uncertainty: hence the comparison with the ocean. We go through this journey by the grace of God.

This is more than a pious expression of faith. Our individual lives as well as all life on earth are sustained by a confluence of countless factors over which we have absolutely no control. Whether it is the appropriate physical conditions of temperature, atmospheric pressure, and percentage of oxygen in the air, or the subtle laws of physics and chemistry that are inexorably at work in our bodies and brain to maintain our physiological and neural well being, we live taking all these for granted. Here the sage-poet not only reminds us of our indebtedness to these unrecognized factors, but by praying for their eternal life he says that all life on earth and the entire universe will exist only as long as their undergirding support-systems do.

When one recites a work like Sivapurāṇam, one seldom reflects on the allusions or inner significance because the goal in such recitations is the associated spiritual experience and not understanding the meanings and contexts. Aside from the spiritual value of reciting a work like this, it is interesting, if not necessary, to note that allusions in sacred literature refer that to the cultural framework of the work.

1.4

ஆகமம் ஆகி நின்று அண்ணிப்பான் தாள் வாழ்க

āgamam āgi-niḍṟu aṇṇippān tāḷ vāzka

May the feet of the One Who became
the Agamas endure for ever!

Word meanings

āgamam - The Āgamas;

āgi ninḍṟu - having become;

aṇṇippān - who approaches, comes near;

tāḷ - feet

vāzga - May (they) live for ever in auspiciousness!

Explanatory reflections

The word *āgamam* refers to any sacred writing in the Hindu, Buddhist, and Jaina traditions. In English the word Scripture (or the Scriptures) means the Old and the New Testaments (the Bible). However, by extension, the word (without the capital) may be used to refer to any sacred writing. In Tamil, *āgamam* generally refers to a Saiva religious texts. The Tamil *āgamas* are not part of the Vedic corpus. Vedic texts are known as *nigamas*. *Āgama* literally means that which has come down, just as *avatāra* refers to the Divine who has come down to earth. Women and Non-Brahmins were not barred from listening to or reciting the *Āgamas*, although it used to said sometimes that Āgamas were not intended for the common people. In Saiva Siddhāntam, the canonical *Āgamas* number twenty-eight.

One may also interpret *Āgamas* metaphorically as scriptural paths to spiritual fulfillment, to Divinity, the right way, as it were. In the Saiva Siddhānta tradition, this right way has been revealed to humankind by none other than the Divine (symbolized as Siva all through this work). Normally one would say that we come close to the Divine by following the spiritual path. But our poet says here that the Divine comes close to us through the spiritual path.

How are we to understand this? A child in need of food or security runs to its mother. More often than not, it is the mother who is caring for the welfare of the child. She does this out of unbounded love. Likewise, we are told here that the Divine transformed itself into the *Āgamas* and has come to us. It is always close to us. The prayer is that it be that way for ever.

Now one might wonder if this is really always so. Is the path of spiritual fulfillment that close to everyone? There are two answers to this question. First, it is certainly the case for those who have received grace, as with the mystic poet Māṇikkavāsakar. Those who are thus blessed feel that the Divine has come to them and remains with them. The other answer is that this is indeed true for everyone, except that not everyone recognizes it. It is somewhat like oxygen which sustains our life, but not everybody breathes it consciously.

1.5

ஏகன் அநேகன் இறைவன் அடி வாழ்க

ēgan anēgan iṟaivan aḍi vāzka

May the feet of the One-Many God endure!

Word meanings

ēgan - one person;

anēgan - multiple-person

iṟaivan - God

aḍi vāzga - May (His) feet endure!

Explanatory reflections

The Divine is but one: ekam sat, it says in the Rig Veda. But the Divine is many in two different ways. First, it is perceived, described, imagined, and proclaimed in countless ways by the various religious traditions of the human family. *Viprā bahudā vadanti*: the learned call it in many ways. In another sense too, God becomes many. Divinity is present in countless beings. Each of us embodies the Divine. God's multiple splendors may be seen in every person and in every living being. (In Tamil, *iṟaivan* is one of many words for God. In classical Tamil it is also referred to by other names, like *sivan, kaḍavuḷ, īsan*.

It is in lines like this that we see the mystic vision which is quite different from theological dogmas. We all see many things, and take them to be as such. The sophisticated physicist who also sees many things, recognizes a unity of laws and basic entities beneath them all. The mystic sees the Many but recognizes not only the One in all, but also a spiritual element in that Unity.

Religions conceptualize God as One. Human beings identify creatures as many. But a deeper (Upanishadic) vision tells us that the Multitude are but splinters of the One. Therefore, it is God Who becomes Many in the world of our experience. We often seek to find unity behind diversity. God does the opposite: Divinity expresses Its unity as diversity. It is somewhat like the same person playing different roles at different times: as child, as spouse, as parent, as student, as teacher, etc. In the *Tiruvempāvai* there is a beautiful verse which says how one became two, two became three, etc., and eventually became many: female, male, neuter, effulgent light, air, earth,…

peṇṇāgi āṇāgi aliyāgip piṟangkoḷichēr
viṇṇāgi maṇṇāgi…..

The many-person aspect of God may be understood by means of an analogy. If we consider music, we find it is impossible to grasp it in the abstract. And yet there are countless manifestations of music in songs and melodies. Like music, God is to be experienced, not conceptualized in many modes and analyzed. That is why the monotheistic mode is abstract, unvisualizable, sometimes even somber, whereas the polytheistic is colorful, rich, full of joy and splendor in its expressions.

2.1

வேகம் கெடுத்தாண்ட வேந்தன் அடி வெல்க

vēgam keḍuttāṇḍa vēndan aḍi velga!

May the feet of the lord who arrested

the speed be victorious!

Word meanings

vēgam - speed

keḍuttu - spoilt, stopped

āṇḍa - (who) ruled

vēndan - king, lord

aḍi - feet

velga - May (they) be victorious!

Explanatory reflections

The mind is a great gift that human beings have received from the Divine. It accomplishes a great many things. Its primary characteristic is that it is never still. It is often restless, it wanders from thought to thought, it is seldom fixed at one point, it is continuously on the move as it were, not unlike a wild horse that is for ever moving very fast.

The goal of yogic exercises is to still the mind. Yoga is union with the Divine. It is the link with the Divine that calms the restless mind. Hence the poet describes the Divine here as the One that puts a break (stops) the speed (restless movement) of the mind.

The idea is that only those who are connected to the Divine, whether through periodic prayers, meditation, or yogic practice, will be able to free themselves from restlessness and the associated strains, Tiruvaḷḷuvar expressed this idea in one of his Kuraḷs (I-7):

> *tanakkuvamai illātān tāḷ cērndrārkku allāl*
> *manakkavalai māṯral aridu.*
>
> Save for who've reached the feet of the Peerless One
> Relief from distress is hard to be done.

We may note here that in the Hindu framework feet have a dual value. The feet of an ordinary person is regarded as his inferior part while his head is the superior. This is because the feet (and the footwear) touch the ground with all its dust and dirt while the head in involved in thoughts. However, the feet of a person we respect: our parents, teacher, and God are venerated. The symbolism is that we regard ourselves as very low compared to the ones whose feet we touch. It is a mark of utter humility.

2.2

பிறப்பறுக்கும் பிஞ்ஞகன்தன் பெய்கழல்கள் வெல்க

piṟappaṟukkum piññagantan peikazalkal velga

Who cuts the cycle of rebirths,

may his boon-giving feet be victorious

Word meanings

piṟappu - birth

aṟukkum - one who cuts off

piññagan- One with the matted hair

tan - His

pei - showering

kazalkaḷ - feet

velga - may (they) be victorious

Explanatory reflections

The soul is passing through the birth- death cycle. This is referred to as *saṃsāra.* Human birth is meant to reap the consequences of karma. Ultimate release or liberation (*moksha*) is when the soul is relieved from this cycle. The goal of spiritual life is to achieve *moksh*a. This may also be attained by grace. That is to say, Divinity may cut off the cycle of *saṃsāra.* In the Saiva framework, Siva is the Divinity.

The word *piññakam* means a hair-dress or plaited hair: *pinnal* in modern Tamil. In puranic imagery, Siva is pictured with matted hair. Hence he is also known as *piññagan,* an epithet by which the poet refers to Him in this line.

The word *kazal* could mean foot or an ankle ring worn by brave warriors. Here, it refers to Shiva's feet which shower all the blessings on us. Hence they are described as *peikazal*: feet that abundantly rain (boons) on us mortals here on earth. One of the boons is precisely the cutting off of the birth-death cycle from which the devotee is striving to be liberated.

The poet's prayer here is that those feet become victorious, in other words that they help the aspirant attain *moksha*. What is remarkable here is that the poet prays for the victory of God's own feet. This may seem to be an unusual mode of praying in that it expresses the wish for the success of the Lord's feet which must be, by definition, omnipotent. This is because those feet are what will help the aspirant in liberation from the birth-death cycle. What the poet is actually praying for is that we may be the beneficiaries of God's generosity in this matter. It is somewhat like recognizing that rain is good for agriculture, and praying that it may fall on our land. Thus the showering that the metaphor is appropriate.

2.3

புறந்தார்க்குச் சேயோன் தன் பூங்கழல்கள் வெல்க

purattārkkuch chēyōn tan pūṅkazalkaḷ velga

May the flowered feet of Him

Who is far from unbelievers be victorious!

Word meanings

puṟattārkku - to strangers

chēyōn tan - of Siva

pūṅkazalkaḷ - flowered feet

velga - may (they) be victorious!

Explanatory reflections

The word *puṟattān* could mean stranger or foreigner (cf. *paradēsi*), or one who is far away. Here it refers to those who are without faith, who reject the transcendental. The poet says that the Divine is far away from such people. More exactly, they have moved themselves far away from the Divine. The name *chēyōn* refers to Skanda, whereas *cheyān* refers to Siva. Here it is simply the Divine.

This line suggests that in the society where our poet lived, not everyone was a God-fearing devotee. The fact that they are mentioned suggests that there were also unbelievers and atheists (Buddhists and Jains?) in those days.

What does one mean by wishing victory of the God? Perhaps the poet is saying that he wishes such people to come under the love and care of the

Divine.

There is an Italian proverb which says: *Assenza nemica di amore*: Absence is the enemy of love. This refers to love between people. Our poet implies more generally that absence of God (i.e. the qualities we associate with God) from one's heart is the enemy of love. It is important to remember in these contexts that many of the lines in Sivapurāṇam become more relevant and meaningful when we interpret Siva as symbol for whatever is positive, noble, and all-embracing in the human spirit.

John Milton spoke of "flowers worthy of Paradise." Our poet sanctifies flowers by associating them with the feet of God. Flowers are soft and fragrant, colorful and beautiful, and they harm no one. Referring to God as One with flowered feet could be to express the idea that when a person accepts God into his heart, that is to say when one assimilates life-giving, life-affirming, and other positive qualities, that would be a soothing and joyous experience rather a harsh intrusion such as would happen when one adopts the opposite traits.

2.4

கரங்குவிவார் உள்மகிழும் கோன்கழல்கள் வெல்க

karaṅkuvivār uḷmagizum kōnkazalgaḷ velga

Of Him whose worship gives inner joy,

may his royal feet they be victorious!

Word meanings

karam - hands

kuvivār - who hold together as a cone

uḷ - (in the) heart

makizum - enjoying

kōn - king

kazal - feet

velga - may (they) be victorious

Explanatory reflections

Sivapurāṇam and other devotional literature are fascinating not only for the intense piety they convey and the metaphysical subtleties they embody, but also for the poetic expressions they use. Thus, here we see the phrase *karam kuvivār*. The word *karam* simply means hand. The word *kuvikkiṟadu* means to become conical, or to bring one's hands together in the form of a cone to express reverence.

The poet says that those who worship God in this way experience an inner delight in their hearts. This is what spiritual ecstasy is all about. Prayer is an effort to recognize and connect with the supreme cosmic principle that undergirds the world and all existence. When that connection is established, not through logic and reason, but from a prayerful merger, one experiences a joy that has no ordinary equivalent. Those who participate in bhajan, in singing psalms, and in chanting hymns in church or synagogue or temple, and who peacefully meditate in silence, surely experience this delight deep in their hearts (*uḷmakizchi*). It is of this that the poet speaks in this line. Again our poet prays for the victory of God's boon-giving feet, by which he means that we may come under their sway. The metaphor of a king emphasizes the fact that this is a gift from God, even as a powerful monarch might (used to) bestow a boon on a common citizen.

We are reminded of Dante's lines (*Purgatory*, XVII):

> All indistinctly apprehend a bliss,
> On which the soul may rest; the hearts of all
> yearn after it.

.

2.5

சிரம்குவிவார் ஓங்குவிக்கும் சீரோன் கழல் வெல்க

chiram kuvivār ōṅguvikkum chīrōn kazal vega

May the feet of the One who uplifts those that bow with their head be victorious!

Word meanings

chiram - head

kuvivār - who hold together as a cone

ōṅguvikkum - who raises, uplkifts

chīrōn - (of) one with splendor

kazal - feet

velga - may (they) be victorious!

Explanatory reflections

People pray to the Lord by bowing their heads as a mark of reverence. By this gesture, they make themselves appropriately low with respect to the Divine. But in turn, God raises them to a higher level. It may seem ironic that by bringing oneself to a less lofty position, one actually reaches an even higher level. This happens because bowing is a sign of humility. Over the ages, humility has been extolled by many. It says in The Christian Bible (James, 4.10): "Humble yourselves before the Lord, and he will exalt you."

According to an old saying which is sometimes attributed to William Cowper:

Rather to bow than break is profitable;
Humility is a thing commendable.

We are also reminded here of John Bunyan's words (*The shepherd boy sings in the valley of humiliation*):

He that is down needs fear no fall,
He that is low, no pride;
He that is humble ever shall
Have God to be his guide.

However, we may remind ourselves at this point that humility need not be shown only towards God or a person who happens to be more powerful than oneself. When an individual with attainments - whether in material wealth, political power, intelligence or renown, encounters people of lesser attainments, he or she could be arrogant or unassuming. In the former instance one goes down in the view of others, and in the latter case, one receives greater respect and admiration, goes even higher in the estimation of the people.

Thus, from the poet's reference to the reward that comes from bowing down to the Divine, namely that one is raised higher, we may learn the value of humility as a virtue, for all too often even people who are reverential to God in temple become arrogant towards those who happen to be in a lower station in life. The value of works like Sivapurāṇam lies not only in their spiritual dimension, but no less in the lessons they teach as to how one should conduct oneself in life.

3.1

ஈசன் அடிபோற்றி எந்தை அடிபோற்றி

īsan aḍipōṯṟi endai aḍipōṯṟi

Praise be unto Siva's feet,

praise be unto my Father's feet!

Word meanings

īsan - God

aḍi - feet

pōṯṟi - praise

endai - my father

aḍi - feet

pōṯṟi - praise

Explanatory reflections

Literally, the word *īsan* is very much like the Sanskrit *īshva*r. It refers to Divinity. However, in Saiva framework, it stands for Lord Siva. In Tamil, one sometimes gives a non-Sanskrit etymology for the word. The word īdal means to give, usually to give to someone at a lower level. Thus īsan could mean one who gives, bestows, etc. Since God is the source of everything, it is God Who gives us everything. Hence God is called īsan.

Likewise, the word *mahēsha* (*mahā īsha*), meaning the great īsha, refers to Lord Siva. In Tamil, the corresponding word makēsan is sometimes interpreted as *makam* (sacrifice) + *īsan* (God): the

God of sacrifice.

The word *endai* is a combination of *en tandai:* my father. Again, here it refers to Lord Siva since he is also regarded as the progenitor of the entire universe. Another Tamil poet exclaimed to God, "*nī enakku vāitta tandai allavō*?" (Art Thou not the father who was made for me?)

In the Tamil religious tradition, as in others, praising the Divine is a mode of paying homage to God. More specifically here, the poet speaks of praising the feet of the Lord. For, in the imagery of the tradition, one receives the grace of God through His feet. So in this and in the next few lines, the poet says, "Praise be unto the feet of Shiva!"

Public and eloquent praising of the great, living or dead, used to be called panegyric or eulogy in ancient Greece. In most religious traditions God is praised in various ways. In the Christian tradition there are the lauds which are hymns of praise to God. In the Vedic tradition we have the stotras which are also liturgical hymns of praise. So in this and the following few lines our poet calls for the praise of Siva with various epithets. One can never err in praising the Divine.

In Shakespeare's *Pericles* we read the lines:

O you gods,

Why do you make us love your goodly gifts,
And snatch them right away?
Here our poet says,
O you God,
Why do you make me love your wondrous nature
And heap praises upon Thee?

3.2

தசேன் அடிபோற்றி சிவன் சவேடி போற்றி

dēsan aḍipōṭṟi sivan chēvaḍipōṭṟi

Praise be unto the Effulgent One's feet, praise be unto Shiva's red feet

Word meanings

dēsan - (of) the effulgent one

aḍipōṭṟi - praise be unto (his) feet

sivan - siva

chēvaḍi - red feet

pōṭṟi - praise!

Explanatory reflections

The word dēsu (Sanskrit, *tejas*) means luster. From this we get dēsan: one who is lustrous, illustrious, the Effulgent One. This is one of many epithets for Shiva. When we speak of light, we must distinguish between three kinds of light. Fist there is physical light: the light that enables us to see things and recognizes colors. This light is essential for our biological existence. It is said in the Book of Genesis that God first commanded light to emerge (yehiy 'or: Fiat lux: et there be light!) in the world. This prompted John Milton to write; Hail, holy light, offspring of Heaven's first-born.

Then there is moral light: This is the light that enables us to see right from wrong, good from bad.

This is the light that prompts us to love and kindness and caring. As Robert Browning wrote (*Stafford*):

> The great beacon light God sets in all,
> The conscience of each bosom.

Finally there is spiritual light. Spiritual light is the vision that enables some to see beyond and beneath the world of terrestrial and physical existence, and become aware of a different level of reality. This awareness of the transcendental constitutes spiritual enlightenment. Spiritual enlightenment comes from the Divine. R. W. Gilder put it this way (*Light: The New Day*):

> Against the darkness outer
> God's light his likeness takes,
> And he from the mighty doubter
> The great believer makes.

Thus when Divinity's spiritual effulgence touches the human heart, the unbeliever is transformed into a believer.

The word *chēvaḍi* literally means *red feet*. Red is an auspicious color in the tradition. That is why the *sindhūr* is red. In esoteric etymology, the *chi* in sivan (chivan) stands for red. In Tamil, *chivappu* means red. The letter *va* stands for the cosmic energy that is an aspect of sivan. We may note that Priyāzvār referred to Vishṇu's feet as red (*avan chēvaḍi chevvi tirukkāppu*). Here the Saiva poet refers to Siva's feet likewise when he pays homage to the Effulgent One, as the One from Whom spiritual light emerges.

3.3

நேயத்தே நின்ற நிமலன் அடி போற்றி

nēyattē ninḍṟa nimalan aḍi pōṭṟi

Praise be unto the feet of the Pure One who stands for all that is good!

Word meanings

neyattē – in (of) good, love

ninḍṟa - who stood for

nimalan - One Who is devoid of impurity

aḍi poṭṟi - praise be unto (His) feet

Explanatory reflections

The Divine is said to possess many good qualities. Indeed the Divine may be pictured as the principle that embodies in limitless measure all that is good and glorious. Of these qualities love is perhaps the loftiest. Here the poet says that the Divine always stands with respect to the bhakta (devotee) with boundless love.

God's mercy is an expression of divine love. Poets and thinkers have called love the essence of God, for ultimately it is the most lofty emotion in the heart of humans. Love gives warmth and feelings of security. Love is at the root of caring and compassion, it forgives and comes to help in times of need, it is the source of deep-felt joy and ecstasy. Do not people of faith and devotion say the same things about the Divine no matter how they name or conceive it? This then is why the poet says that the Loving One had always stood by the devotee. We often extol people who are pure of heart. "Blessed are the pure of heart," it says in the New Testament, "for they shall see God." But what does one mean by pure of heart? One means being without any blemish. It means being perfect in every way.

Can a mortal be so pure? Recall Pascal's dictum *Les choses valent toujours mieux dans leur source,* often translated as "The stream is always purer at its source." This may be said of the stream of life too: Its source is purer than it itself is. We may think of God as perfection, as the purest of whatever is pure. So the poet refers to the Divine as the One who is pure.

There is love in the human heart also, but it is never completely spotless, for nothing that is human is ever perfect. We are reminded of Francis Bacon's line in *Advancement of Learning* where he said that "the sun which passeth through pollutions, itself remains as pure." In the Hindu framework we may say that that supreme consciousness (*paramātman*) passes through many impurities in its manifestations as individual conscious entities (*jivātmans*), and yet retains its own purity. In this line the poet refers to the Divine as the supreme aspect of love and of purity: That is to say, of a love that is without blemish. Again and again, in the lines of the Sivapurāṇam we are made aware of some of the countless features of the Supreme. That is what grand devotional poetry does.

3.4

மாயப் பிறப்பு அறுக்கும் மன்னன்
அடி போற்றி

māyap pi̱rappu a̱rukkum mannan aḍipōṭṟi

Praise be unto the feet of Him

Who cuts off illusive birth

Word meanings

māya - illusory

pi̱rappu - birth

a̱rukkum - (who) cuts off

mannan - king

aḍipōṭṟi - praise be unto (His) name.

Explanatory reflections

There are two principal levels of reality: the ephemeral and the permanent. The ephemeral level of reality is called *māyā,* often translated as *illusion,* though the term has many philosophically more subtle interpretations. In simple terms, by *māyā* one means that reality at the ephemeral level is a temporal phenomenon with no ultimate significance.

In the course of our everyday life we experience a variety of things. Our normal consciousness gives us the impression that these experiences are all real, that they are there to stay for ever. In fact, however, every bit of experience soon fades into an irrevocable past, lingers in our own, and then in some others' memories. Eventually they all dissolve into nothingness. This is why it is regarded as mere illusion, no more substantial in the long run than last night's dream while we were asleep.

Thus, it is maintained, the journey of human life itself is one grand illusion. Every night we go to sleep and are subjected to a series of dreams, we take different births and have a series of passingexperiences. When we wake up, we realize that it was all just dreams, and the real world is very different from that dream-world. Likewise, declare the Hindu seers, this world which we take to be real is another level of illusion. This realization comes with spiritual awakening.

When that spiritual awakening occurs, one is no longer subject to the illusion-generating cycle of re-birth and re-death. In this line, the poet declares that we get that awakening and the resulting redemption from *saṃsāra* (birth-death cycle) by the grace of the Divine. Hence Divinity is described here as the One Who cuts off the illusory cycle. For without the Grace of God we can never attain spiritual enlightenment, and without spiritual enlightenment we are condemned to repeat the re-incarnation cycle. The idea is that *moksha* which is equivalent to release from re-birth and merger with the Divine happens by the grace of God; or rather it is God's grace that serves as an instrument for this. More generally, every good fortune that comes to us may be regarded as a grace from God, for no matter what we think we do to obtain it, there are factors beyond our will and capacity that enable to achieve it.

3.5

சீரார் பெருந்துறை நம் தேவன்
அடி போற்றி

cīrār perundu_rai namdēvan aḍi pōṯṟi

Praise to the feet of

the splendid One of Perundu_rai

Word meanings

cīrār - the One with splendor

perundu_rai - name of a place

nam - our (my)

dēvan - God

aḍipōṯṟi - praise unto (HIs) feet

Explanatory reflections

In this line there is an allusion to Maṅikkavāsagar's own life. It recalls the incident in which he stopped at the town of Perundurai during a royal mission to acquire some horses for the king. It was here that he heard the chanting of a mantra of Lord Shiva at the Avuḍaiyār temple. This experience transformed his life completely, for he received blessings from a sage sitting under a tree. It was here that the poet is said have uttered the first verse of Tiruvācakam, and the first mantra of Sivapurāṇam. It was thus that Vadavūrar came to be called Māṇikkavāsagar.

The temple of Periya Āvuḍaiyār still stands there

on the banks of River Shanmuga. Here may be seen a liṅgam which is believed to be a *svayambhū*: that is, that it was formed by itself. The icon (*mūrti*) here is also known as *peru-uḍaiyār*: One who has greatness, grandeur (*perumai*). (In Sanskrit: *brihadīshvar*.)

Because the poet received his enlightenment here, in this context he refers to the Divine as *nam dēvan* (our God, אֱלֹהֵינוּ, where the *our* is a poetic *our*, meaning my). But I see a deeper significance here. Whereas most people of faith adopt the deities of their group and background, some have their own vision of the transcendent. In principle, each searcher has his/her own revelation. In that sense, God is an indefinable personal experience. When the poet speaks of our God, he does not simply mean my God in the poetic-royal sense, but that every one of us has a profound my-God experience. These experiences need not, indeed often are not, the same. For whatever the Divine is, we get but a glimpse of it in the mortal frame. Sugusta Arnold Ward wrote (*Robert Elsmere*) that "Truth has never been, can never be, contained in any one creed." It is equally true that God has never been, can never be, contained in any one form. This is the significance of the term, "my God."

Indeed, this is one of the greatest religious

visions of humanity. It is, as of now, uniquely Hindu, even though it is not always internalized by all who call themselves Hindus. But I like to think that in due course the faithful of all religions, and of all sects and subsects within religions with their diverse doctrinal views will adopt this principle of *polyodosism*: multiple paths for spiritual fulfillment.

4.1.

ஆராத இன்பம் அருளும் மலை போற்றி

ārāda inbam aruḷum malai pōṭṟi

Praise be unto the mountain that bestows
the grace of non-satiating joy!

Word meanings

ārāda - that which never makes us satiated

inbam - joy, pleasure

aruḷum - Who graces

malai - mountain

pōṭṟi - praise be unto (it)

Explanatory reflections

Delight or joy is known as *inbam* in Tamil. Even the best of delights are such that we can only take so much of them. It is important to distinguish between physical pleasure and spiritual joy. The Latin poet Cicero said: *Omnibus in rebus voluptatibus maximis fastidium finitimum est*: In all things aversion follows the greatest pleasures. That is to say, sooner or later, one becomes satiated with any pleasure to the point of being fed up with it. However, notes the poet here, one can never tire of the joy that comes from God-realization. That is what is meant by the term *ārāda inbam*. No matter how much of it we experience, we will never feel we have had enough of it. And even if we wanted a joy to last, it will not.

John Norris wrote in *The Parting*:

How fading are the joys we dote upon!
Like apparitions seen and gone.
But those which soonest take their flight
Are the most exquisite and strong,--
Like angels' visits, short and bright;
Mortality 's too weak to bear them long.

But how does one get this *ārāda inbam*? Not by seeking, nor even by trying hard, but, we are told, it is by the grace of the Divine that one comes to it. That is how our poet received it. He was, we recall, on a very worldly mission: to buy horses for the king. Quite unexpectedly, he heard the name of Lord Shiva, and this led him to the sage, and thus did he receive spiritual illumination. Overwhelmed by the magnificence of the Divine, our poet describes it metaphorically as a mountain.

We are reminded of Gerald Massey's verse in *The Bridgegroom of Beauty*:

Not by appointment do we meet Delight
And Joy; they heed not our expectancy.
But round some corner in the streets of life.
They, on a sudden, clasp us with a smile.

4.2

சிவன் அவன் என்சிந்தையுள் நின்ற அதனால்

sivan avan en chindaiyuḷ ninḍṟa adanāl

Because he, Sivan, remains in my mind

Word meanings

sivan - Lord Shiva

avan - He

en - my

chindaiyuḷ - mind

ninḍṟa - stayed

adanāl - therefore

Explanatory Reflections

One may wonder what prompted the poet to create the work he has created. There could be any number of reasons why a writer composes a work. He/she may have been given an assignment to do it. He/she may want to compete for a prize. He/she may desire to get fame and name. He/she may hope to make money out of it. He/she has an urge to write something. One can go on and on.

Why do we talk about anything at all? Because it is in our mind. When that which is in our mind is lofty and fulfilling, we cannot but help share it with others. They are truly blessed whose minds are with such things. In this line our poet conveys the joy he feels by the constant presence of God in it. We may note in passing that the word *chindai* in Tamil is derived from the Sanskrit *chinta*, and it could also mean thought or concept. *Chindaicheivadu* means to meditate. We are reminded of the lines, attributed to the 16th century poet, Edward Dyer (*Still*):

> My mind to me a kingdom is,
> Such present joys therein I find,
> As far exceeds all earthly bliss,
> That God or Nature hath assign.

In other words, there is a happy experience that comes from what is in the mind that material things cannot afford. When powerful ideas come to mind, it is difficult to subdue or expel them. Alfred de Musset said: *Malgrē moi, l'infini me tourmente*: In spite of myself, infinity torments me. So it is here: God is always present in his mind, whether he wills it or not. This does not torment him, it inspires him, it moves him to ecstasy such as no other thought or theme could.

4.3

அவன் அருளாலே அவன் தாள் வணங்கி

avan aruḷālē avan tāḷ vaṇaṅgi

By His grace, having paid homage to His feet

Word meanings

avan - His

aruḷālē - from grace

avan - His

tāḷ - feet

vaṇaṅgi - having paid homage to

Explanatory reflections

The poet has been paying homage to Lord Shiva. But he takes no special credit for this. He does not imagine that he has been devoted to the Lord because of his own special qualities. He does not claim that he is unlike other ordinary people, and therefore exceptional in his extreme commitment to the Lord. Rather, he gives the whole credit for this to the Divine. He declares that it is because of God's grace that he is able to be so utterly devoted to Him.

This is not just an interesting stance to take, it has a profound meaning. All too often people take pride in their accomplishments, and often rightly so. Whether a student passes an exam successfully, or one gets promoted in one's job for good performance, or one receives the Nobel Prize, or whatever, it is true that every significant achievement is the result of hard work, total dedication, self-discipline, and the like. So, one is entitled to the self-congra-tulation in which the achiever indulges.

But we may ask: Why is it that one person turns out to be hard working, self-disciplined, unperturbed by distractions, etc., and another is plain lazy and without any eagerness to do well and succeed, let alone exceptionally bright or gifted? Ultimately, in scientific terms, we may trace the causes for successes to genes, upbringing, etc. But where do these come from? Why is one endowed with the right kind of genes in the right kind of place and family while another is not? One traditional explanation for this is that this is due to our previous karma, results of actions in a previous birth. Another is that the blessing from grace (*aruḷ*). The poet says it was because of that grace that he became a person who worshiped Shiva so much. In truth, there is very little that we can call our own. Invariably all the good things we receive in life are blessings: gifts from God without which we could be in dire straits.

Grace is a complex theological concept, with varying interpretations in different religions and within sects and subsects within the same religion.

In the Christiantradition, Catholics generally hold that one gets grace by accepting Christ. It used to be believed in the Middle Ages that those who don't deserve that grace as a result of committing serious sins can get it by paying the Church a certain amount. The Pope would then grant them what was called an *indulgence*. In the year 1527 Martin Luther rebelled against the idea of buying grace, and this was the starting of the Protestant reformation.

In the Hindu tradition, it is believed that God gives grace (*anugraha, aruḷ*) to two kinds of people: to those who strive to get it by reaching out to God, and sometimes to those who don't seek Him voluntarily. From among those who do not seek, God chooses some and gives them grace. The philosopher-saint Madhvacharya did not subscribe to this view, asserting that only those who work for it receive it.

4.4

சிந்தை மகிழச் சிவ புராணம் தன்னை

chindai magiz sivapurāṇam tannai

The mind-delighting Sivapurāṇam

Word meanings

chindai - mind

magiz - enjoying

sivapurāṇam – Sivapurāṇam

tannai - it

Explanatory Reflections

We like to do things that are satisfying to us. We read stories, we watch movies, and play games, and do many other things that add color to life and bring us joy. Likewise we read or recite poetry, or sing hymns to God because these too bring us deep fulfillment.

In this line the poet says that an important feature of Sivapurāṇam is that it makes us rejoice. The word *magizvadu*: to rejoice, is a beautiful word in Tamil. It conveys a sense of deep-felt joy. A word for husband in classical poetic Tamil is *magiznan*: one who gives or brings joy.

One may find it strange that the poet describes his own work as bringing joy. One may wonder: Should this not be the role of a reader or a literary critic to say this? At first this may seem to be so. However, we must remember that this is not like a painting done by an artist or a poem written in the usual mode. Rather, this is a work of supreme inspiration, like a revelation. The poet does not sit down and think of what would be the next good line to formulate. The work flows from his lips even as nectar flows from a flower. That is why he came to be called Māṇikkavāsagar. He does not regard himself as the original author of the work, but merely as an instrument of God through whom the composition is conveyed to the people.

Then again, we note that he is speaking of joy to the mind rather than to the heart. Should not religious ecstasy be a matter for the heart rather than for the mind? Not necessarily. It is true that in meditation and in devotional singing where meaning and words matter less than deep absorption, joy is more experiential than analytical. However, in poetry and philosophy there is thought and reflection. These are matters for the mind. In fact, later in the work, the poet brings out the tenets of Saiva Siddhāntam. It certainly belongs to the realm of the mind.

Here we are reminded of the Psalm 94.19 where it says:

> In the multitude of my thoughts within me,
> your comforts delight my soul"

In his classic commentary on this Albert Barnes wrote:

> And yet, in this multitude of thoughts (that cross the mind) - so empty, so foolish, so sinful, so vexing, so skeptical, so polluting - ... there are thoughts of God, ... of heaven, of hope, of faith, of love, of benevolence; thoughts within us, when the divine promises come to the heart, and the prospect of heaven warms the soul.

4.5

முந்தை வினைமுழுதும் ஓய உரைப்பன் யான்

mundai vinai muzudum ōya uraippan yān

To erase the effects of all past I will chant

Word meanings

mundai - former

vinai - actions

muzudum - whole of, all

ōya - (so that they may) cease

uraippan - will utter, will speak

yān - I

Explanatory Reflections

This line has reference to the law of *karma* which is part of the Hindu spiritual framework. The poet recognizes that his current birth is a consequence of his actions and attitudes in a previous birth. The term *mundai vinai* literally means former actions, and here it refers to deeds done in a previous birth.

In the Hindu view, every will bear fruit sooner or later, in this or in another birth. By this one means that aside from the effect on others, our actions also affect us. This is what *karma* is all about. It is to reap this kārmic consequence on ourselves that we are re-born.

Therefore, if we can somehow erase kārmic

consequences, there will not be re-birth. That is to say, we will attain moksha or merger with the Supreme. Such *moksha* may be achieved by one of several modes: total renunciation of everything worldly, total dedication to the Divine, pursuing a completely spiritual path, etc.

Our poet says here that he will be uttering the Sivapurāṇam to erase the effects of his previous deeds. By his devotional homage to Sihva through this grand composition he will rid himself of the burden that would otherwise force him to another birth.

The significance of this line is that it reflects the possible impact of the work. It reminds us that when this work is read in the spirit of a true devotee of Shiva (*Shivabhakta*), it can have enormous spiritual value. It is a matter of common experience that when we read a good book, sing or listen to a beautiful song, or chant a prayer with devotion, it transforms us. This transformation can occur on the intellectual, moral, epistemological, or spiritual plane. We may learn from this line that reading or reciting Sivapurāṇam will have such a spiritually transformational effect on us. We are reminded here of the words of St. John of Ladder who said (15:61),

Lovers of God are moved to spiritual joy, to

> divine love, and to tears both by worldly and by religious songs.

In this context we may also recall the words of St. John Chrysostom (*On Psalm*):

> Even if you do not understand the meaning of the words, for the time being teach your mouth to say them, for the tongue is sanctified by the words alone whenever it says them with good will.

5.1

கண் நுதலான் தன்கருணைக் கண்காட்ட வந்து எய்தி

kaṇṇudalān tan karuṇai kaṇkāṭṭavandu eidi

The Three-eyed One having come

with His merciful glance

Word meanings

kaṇ - eye

nudal - forehead

kaṇnudalān - One with an eye of his fore- head (Lord Shiva)

tan - his

karuṇai - compassion, mercy

kaṇ - eye

kāṭṭa - to show

vandu - having come

eidi - approached

Explanatory reflections

The term *kaṇnudalān* is one of the countless names for Lord Siva in the Tamil tradition. It means One who has an eye on his forehead. The reference therefore is to Siva's Third Eye which has stutendous powers. The Third Eye has occult significance. There is reference to it in Gnosticism, Buddhism, mystical Christianity, and other esoteric systems also.

The poet states in this line that Lord Siva came and approached him. Why did He do it? To show mercy on this poor sinner. As we have seen before, in this framework it is through grace, rather than as kārmic reward, that one achieves spiritual enlightenment. It might be argued that grace itself is a result of previous good *karma,* that grace comes only to those who have led a very meritorious life. However, the word *karuṇai* means clemency and mercy in the context of a judging authority. The poet thus recognizes that he has many actions to answer for. He implies by the use of this word that he may well have done things for which he deserves to be punished. That is why he regards grace as a sign of mercy. He feels that the Lord has absolved him of his mistakes, and blessed him with the grace that enables him to recite with ease a work of such great spiritual significance. Recall St. Augustine's statement (*The City of God*): The law detects, grace alone conquers sin." In this view grace is bestowed upon a chosen few.

In the works of great poets who write on their culture, there are many allusions to the literary and cultural framework of the people. In a little known Purāṇic episode (*Shiva Puraṇa: Rudra Samhita,* Section V) Pārvati once teased Siva by covering His two eyes. When this happened, it is said, her hands became moist by emanations from Shiva's third eye, and thus was born a blind demon by the name of Andhika. Since the two eyes of Siva represent the sun and the moon, the result of Pārvati's frolic was to plunge the universe into total darkness. At this moment Lord Shiva, out of compassion for the world, opened His eyes. From this act of mercy on the part of Siva, light was restored in the universe. Some scholars have suggested that this line alludes to that Purāṇic episode.

5.2

எண்ணுதற்கு எட்டா எழில்ஆர் கழல் இறைஞ்சி

eṇṇudaṟku eṭṭā ezilār kazal iṟaiñji

Bowing reverentially to the feet
of the unreachable beautiful One

Word meanings

eṇṇudaṟku - to thinking

eṭṭā - unreachable

ezil ār - (of) the Beautiful One

kazal - (to the) feet

iṟaiñji - bowing down in reverence

Explanatory Reflections

Much of what we do in life is based on thinking. Thought is what sustains the world. It plays an important role as much in everyday matters as in the intellectual realm. Indeed, most of the time, there is very little we can do without thought.

Yet, there are situations where thought is not essential. When we are enjoying good music or tasty food, it is not necessary to be thinking. Oscar Wilde noted that "Beauty ends where an intellectual expression begins." When we try to formulate deep experiences in words, we seldom convey the depth of the experience.

Philosophers, theologians, and religious heads

have been talking about God. Some of their thoughts are beautiful and insightful. But even the most profound thoughts about God barely touch what God actually is. The reason for this, our poet states in this line, is that God is beyond thought. That is to say, God cannot be reached through thought processes. Like music or honey God must be experienced, not analyzed.

The poet who has been touched by God in the depths of his soul, has had a vision of the Divine. He describes God as possessing *ezil* (beauty). He is overwhelmed and as per the tradition, he bows down to express his reverence for the Divine. In this line we see that our poet is conveying a profound understanding born of intense personal experience.

"The mind soars to the lofty," wrote William Hazlitt in an essay. Our poet says, no matter how high it soars it cannot comprehend the fullness of the Divine, for God is beyond the mind's grasp. In other words, divine ecstasy can never be achieved through logic and books.

5.3

விண் நிறைந்தும் மண் நிறைந்தும் மிக்காய், விளங்கு ஒளியாய்

viṇ ni̱raindum maṇ ni̱raindu mikkāi,
viḷangu oḷiyāi
Filling air and land and shining grandly

Word meanings

viṇ - air, atmosphere, cloud
ni̱raindu - filled with
maṇ - earth
ni̱raindu - filled
mikkāi - having become great, superior
viḷangu - shining
oḷiyāi - (as) light, radiance

Explanatory Reflections

The Divine principle is not located here or there, just in temples and in altars, or up in high starry heaven. Rather it is immanent, all pervading, omnipresent. There is not a spot in the universe where the it is not present. Every nook and niche is packed to the full with the Divine.

This is the idea the poet conveys here. Shiva fills the whole atmosphere, i.e. every region above ground. He also fills up every region here below. It is interesting that the poet does not simply say God is here or there, but that every place is filled with (*ni̱raindu*) with the Divine. The expression makes us feel there is a richness and overwhelming abundance of the spiritual in the gross material world. Physical light illumining land and air. That light is the manifestation of God.

But we may see something more in this line. The immanence of Divinity is something that the poet clearly feels within. From such a feeling comes an enlightenment that is beyond worldly knowledge. It is the enlightenment that the poet proclaims. That is why the poet not only mentions God's presence everywhere, but also declares that the Divine is manifest as cosmic effulgence.

The Tamil word *oḷi* has also another meaning: something hidden. Could it be that the poet also meant to say that the earth and air and all the rest of the physical world are places where the Divine is hiding, that is to say that Divinity is occult. Yet, we are told, it is shining everywhere. How can this be? This is so because every aspect of nature is the Divine in a manifested form. It is only when one attains spiritual enlightenment that the hiding place is transformed into the light that is the Divine.

From this perspective, everything has a visible and directly perceivable aspect, as well as a hidden unseen aspect. The latter is the spiritual component of the world. We see here how the mystic's vision arises through connection with something beynd our material life and experience.

5.4

எண் இறந்த எல்லை இலாதானே நின் பெருஞ்சீர்

eṇ iṟanda ellai ilādānē nin peruñchīr

Oh fully great One

beyond the limits of thought

Word meanings

eṇ iṟanda – beyond thought

ellai – limit, boundary

ilādānē - one who is without

nin - your

perum - full

chīr - greatness

Explanatory Reflections

The word *eṇṇuvadu* has several meanings: to think, to guess, to consider, to deliberate, etc. It also means *to count*. Tamil is one of the few languages language (I am aware of) where the same word is used for both thinking and counting. It is somewhat like the word *to reckon* in English which could mean both to guess and to calculate.

In this line, the poet addresses the Divine as one with no limits or boundaries in the world of thought. Thus, no matter how extensive and profound our thoughts, they can never cover all that Divinity includes. There are no boundaries when one envisages God.

Then again, if we take the meaning of counting in the word *eṇṇudal,* then *eṇṇukku ellai illādān* could be taken to mean one who is limitless in the counting of his qualities. In other words, if one tries to count God's qualities, one will discover that this is impossible since the number of God's qualities is literally infinite.

How does one discover this? It is one thing to take this as a proposition because that is what spiritual leaders tell us; this seems reasonable. But it is an entirely different thing to discover this truth first-hand by actually trying to do this. Not many succeed in this, as our poet has.

Our poet did not realize this spiritual truth by repeating what he had heard, nor by reading books on the subject but through grace.

5.5

பொல்லா வினையேன் புகழுமாறு
ஒன்று அறியேன்

pollā vinaiyēn pugazumāṟu ondru aṟiyēn

As one of evil deeds,

I do not know how to laud (the Lord)

Word meanings

pollā - evil

vinaiyēn - one with (such) acts

pugazumāṟu - to praise, to laud

onḍṟu - that one

aṟiyēn - I don't know

Explanatory Reflections

In Tamil literary tradition, great authors usually present at the beginning of their work a formal statement expressing humility, often stating that they are not fully qualified to undertake a work of such significance. This part of the preface is known as *avaiaḍakkam*: modest expression.

In the *avaiaḍakkam* of *Kamba Rāmāyāṇam*, for example, Kamban - perhaps the greatest of all Tamil poets - pleads with scholars not to take the work of "fools, madmen, and deranged devotees" like himself seriously.

In this and the following lines (*avaiaḍakkam*) our poet declares that his previous evil deeds have made him utterly incapable of composing the work because it is impossible for one like himself to engage in pious activities. Because of his past misdeeds he does not have the credentials or the capacity praise the Divine: only those who are pure of heart can truly laud the Lord. If this is not modesty, what is!

It is not unlike the situation in the world of science where unless one has equipped oneself with the appropriate knowledge-background one is not qualified to pass value judgments on a scientific work. Except that here, few are more capable than our poet on this matter.

We could interpret this line to mean the following: Though the Sivapuṟāṇam may be read by anyone at any time, in order to fully appreciate it, and more importantly, in order to benefit from its reading, we need to be pure of heart, free from the sins and passions that add to the burdens of life. This is an important insight that the poet gives us.

Religious works are not the same as literary compositions. To derive full benefit from them, the reader should be mentally and spiritually prepared, i.e. cleansed of evil thoughts and effects, if one is to derive the full benefits from it.

In the tradition, one takes a bath before entering

a temple. Though one only cleans the body of its impurities, it is symbolic of a cleansing of the mind also. Entering a place of worship with impure thoughts is also sacrilegious. So it is when one approaches sacred poetry.

6.1.

புல்லாகிப் பூடாய்ப் புழுவாய் மரமாகி

pullāgi pūḍāi puzuvāi maramāgi
After becoming grass, shrub, worm,
and tree

Word meanings

pullāgi - having become grass
pūḍu - small plant
āi - having become
puzu - a worm
āi - having become
maram - a tree
āgi - having become

Explanatory Reflections

There are in the world countless life forms at various levels of development. In the Hindu framework of reincarnation (*saṃsāra*) there is a soul in all of these. We who are humans today could well have been in some other lifeform in previous births. In the next few lines the poet reflects on some of these through which has gone through.

If we ask a Hindu to name a few lifeforms he/she might have had in earlier incarnations, it is very unlike that any of the ones mentioned here would be mentioned.

Our poet says that he was once a blade of grass.

Grass is perhaps the most abundant and widespread botanical entities in the world. Whether in dense forests or in agricultural lands, in manicured lawns or on mountain slopes, grass finds its way one way or another. To have been a blade of grass is to have been as common and as all over as one can imagine. Grass serves to reap sun's warmth in the soil. The poet's invocation to God even as grass reminds us of the last stanza on the poem *The Voice of Grass* by Sarah Roberts Boyle, which reads:

> Here I come creeping, creeping everywhere;
> My humble song of praise
> Most joyfully I raise
> To Him at whose command
> I beautify the land,
> Creeping, silently creeping everywhere.

Pūḍu refers to any small plant, such as a shrub. In a way it represents a slightly more advanced botanical species. Then the poet speaks of a worm (*puzu*). It seems a lowly lifeform, but the earthworm is a most valuable creature for keeping the soil loose. Next the poet mentions the tree (*maram*). From a generalized perspective of transmigration of souls, this is not an impossibility either. We may note here that all the creatures to which the poet refers are extremely valuable members of the ecosystem.

The poet thinks of these creatures at the lower rungs of the evolutionary ladder as his various previous incarnations. This reflects the poet's breadth of vision. In a remarkable way, it foresees an insight that the scientific world was to formulate centuries later: namely, that we ourselves have evolved from the most pristine forms of life.

6.2

பல் விருகமாகிப் பறவையாய்ப் பாம்பாகி

pal virukamāgi pa<u>r</u>avaiyāi pāmbāgi
After being a prairie dog, bird,
and snake.

Word meanings

pal - many species
virugam - wild dog
āgi - having become
pa<u>r</u>avai - bird
āi - becoming
pāmbu - serpent
āgi - having become

Explanatory Reflections

Now the poet speaks of a stage when he had been born as a wild dog roaming the fields, mindless and fierce, aimless and of no great worth. Humans can also be in such states. In the ancient world, dogs were said to be *silvis aspera*: fierce in the woods. Though in mytho-logy dog is sometimes represented as a companion to the virtuous, classical Hindu society generally regarded dogs as unclean and of low birth, as reflected in this line.

Then there is the picture of being born as bird. We may picture a bird in many ways: as a happy creature soaring in the air, as a joyous singer in the sky, as a little biped with no worries at all. Or again, perhaps, as Charles Lamb wrote (*Crumbs to the Birds*):

> A bird appears as a thoughtless thing…
> No doubt he has his little cares,
> And very hard he often fares,
> The which he patiently bears.

In any event, it is still a life with no ultimate goals, an existence that persists for a while and then passes without a recognition of God.

And then there is the serpent. Renowned in many cultures, but seldom doing anything good for our own lives. Though worshiped here and there, serpents are also dreaded, for they remind us of their venom. So we speak of persons with evil intentions as serpents that creep in the grass, hidden from our view, only to sting when we pass by them.

The poet says in these lines that in past lives he was wild and wandering as a dog, easy going and indifferent to loftier truths as the bird, perhaps stingingly harsh on others like the deadly serpent.

6.3

கல்லாய் மனிதராய்ப் பேயாய்க் கணங்களாய்

kallāi manidarāi pēyāi kaṇaṅgalāi

After being stones, humans, mean spirits, petty beings

Word meanings

kal - stone

āi - becoming

manidar - men, humans

āi - becoming

pēi - fiend, evil spirit

āi - becoming

kaṇaṅgal - petty beings

āi - becoming

Explanatory Reflections

Prior even to life forms there have been rocks and stones in the world. So, before becoming an animate entity, one could well have been an inert stone, or mere molecules that were potentially the building blocks of like as we know it. Thus, this line could refer metaohorically to a life that is thoughtless, mindless, purposeless, and meaningless: physical existence with utterly no sensitivity. Abraham Cowley wrote (*Davideis.* Bk. III):

Stones of small worth may lie unseen by day,
But night itself does the rich gem betray.

Likewise, in this case, the stone of small worth evolved at a different time to become the great realized soul. This thought is to suggest that the potential in each one of us, however lowly at this moment, is unimaginable and unlimited. Then there are discernable human forms. We pass through countless births and deaths as human beings here and there, doing all sorts of things, reaping the fruits, sweet and bitter, of our various actions. The poet is aware of this too.

In the Hindu framework, as in many ancient systems, there exist spirits, disembodied entities that wander the wilderness. Some of these are evil. They are consumed by ill will towards others. They are known as in Tamil as *pēi*. The poet says he has gone through that phase of existence also. Here we may recall Thomas Carlyle's words (*Natural Supernaturalism*):

"... it is mysterious, it is awful to consider that we not only carry a future Ghost within us; but are, in every deed Ghosts!"

The word *kaṇam* (plural: *kaṇaṅgal*) may also connote countless paltry beings in the vast uni-verse where a million wondrous things transpire. Thus the poet says he had also been born previously as so many trivial creatures serving.

The word *kaṇa* (Sanskrit *gaṇa*) has several connotations. It particular, it referred to a variety of semi-divine beings, or followers of such. It was also a name for the disciples of particular spiritual leaders. Here it could be taken to mean simply an ordinary member of some large collection of servants of a revered master. Incidentally, one etymology of the name of Lord *Gaṅesha* is: *Gaṇa* + *Īsha*: God of the *Gaṇas*. Likewise *Gaṇapati* means Chief of the Gaṇas.

6.4

வல் அசுரர் ஆகி முனிவராய்த் தேவராய்ச்

vallasurarāgi munivarāi dēvarāi

After becoming powerful asuras, sages,
divine beings

Word meanings

val - powerful

asurar - asura

āgi - having become

munivar - muni

āi - becoming

dēvar - deva

āi - becoming

Explanatory Reflections

Now the poet recalls that he had taken birth as powerful asuras. In the Rig Veda, the name *asurā* sometimes referred to the Supreme Spirit (like the Ahura of the Zend Avesta). But later, as in the Atharva Veda, it came to denote people who were inimical to the Vedic tradition. In the Hindu mythic framework, there are two types of supernatural beings: those that are allies of the Divine, and those that are unfriendly to it. The first of these are known as devas, and the second came to be called *asuras* (etymologically, those that did not drink the inebriating *sūra*). The notion that there are forces in the world that are against all that is good is fairly common in all religious thought. Thus all religious traditions had corresponding evil spirits, like the *shedu* of the Babylonians, the *daemons* and *Satan* of Judeo-Chrisianity, and the *jinns* of the Islamic world.

In these lines the poet remembers being an *asurā* sometimes, and also a *deva* at other times. This could be interpreted to mean that in some births he was inclined to be pious, and in others he was impious. For each time we are born, we come with different natures, though there may be traces of previous characteristics. That is the mystery of genetic variations.

Generally speaking, *muni* refers to an ascetic who is also a man of wisdom. The word is derived from the Sanskrit *maunam* which means silence. Originally, therefore, a *muni* was a sage who adhered to complete silence. He would not even communicate through gestures or grimaces what he wished to have. Complete silence has its spiritual value which is why it is practiced in meditation and by many religious orders. The Quakers and other religious groups recognize this as part of their practice. The Latin poet Ovid said: *Qui silet, est firmus*: He who is silent is strong. There is an ancient saying: Let us be silent for so are the gods.

In these lines the poet remembers his births as beings that aided and attacked the Divine, and as wise men who spent their whole lives in silent contemplation. The path to realization meanders through many twists and turns. The evolution to the highest form has to go through many modes and melodies of life-forms, some beautiful and some ugly.

6.5

சலெ்லாஅ நின்ற இத் தாவர சங்கமத்துள்

cellā a ninḍṟa ittāvara chaṅgamattuḷ

In all moving or unmoving living things

which stood, in that stable union

Word meanings

cellā - not moving

a - or

ninḍṟa - which stood

i - this

tāvara - foundational, stable

chaṅgam - junction, union

attuḷ - in that

Explanatory Reflections

There are countless kinds of living organisms in the world. They may be, indeed they have been since very ancient times, put into a variety of categories by biological taxonomists. In the traditional Hindu way of categorizing living entities, one speaks of creatures that move (such as fish, animals, insects, birds, etc.) and things that do not (such as plants and trees). The classical scientific writer and physician Charaka (2nd century C.E.) described plants as *sthāvara* or stationary things. Animals are known as *jangama* or moving things. The term is also used for some wandering monks.

Both moving and stationary life forms constitute the basis of all life on the planet. Thus, if one is to take a form of life on earth, one has to belong to one of these two classes of beings. In this line, the poet says that in previous births his soul had been inside both types of living organisms. In this concluding line of his listing of previous births, the poet says essentially that he had been born earlier as every imaginable creature on the planet. Aside from its spiritual connotation, such a reflection establishes in our own minds a deep kinship with all creatures great and small, and instills in us the view that we are, one and all, members of the same family of life on earth.

In the Western tradition, Aristotle was the first to classify plants and animals. In the eighteenth century Carolus Linnaeus laid the foundations of modern taxonomy. It may be noted in passing that in ancient India there was a thorough and extensive classification of plants and animals. The Sanskrit scholar William Jones is said to have remarked that "Linnaeus would probably have adopted the Hindu method had he known the Sanskrit language."

Another way of looking at these reflections is as follows: Consider our current phase of understanding and spiritual development. We have reached it after going through many long and winding routes. Each one of us was at one time a mere child, at one time unlettered, uninformed, immature and ignorant. These may be regarded as our previous avatāras. And now we are in this phase of better understanding and greater enlightenment. One may take that as the idea that the poet conveys here.

7.1

எல்லாப் பிறப்பும் பிறந்து இளைத்தேன், எம்பெருமான்

ellāp piṟappum piṟandiḷaittēn emperumān

I became tired of taking all births, my Lord

Word meanings

ellā - all

piṟappum - and births

piṟandu - being born

iḷaittēn - I grew tired

en - my

perumān - great prince, lord

Explanatory Reflections

The stanza consisting of lines 26 to 31 is one of the most beautiful passages of this work. It reminds us of the traditional Hindu framework of reincarnation in which we are born and born and born again, to live and die and die again, until we become one with that from which we sprang. That ultimate merger is the final emancipation from the birth-death cycle, and is the fruit of spiritual awakening.

There are compensations in terrestrial life, such as passing pleasures and fleeting joys. But there are also pains and sufferings that invariably accompany all this. Moreover, even if it is all only good, the sheer repetitiveness of it all can become exhausting.

The poet, in his profound love for the Supreme, cries out to the Almighty that he is really tired of all this life and death and rebirth. Enough of it all! he is exclaiming.

One of the many names for Shiva is *perumān*. (Vishṇu is known in the Tamil Vaish-ṇava tradition as *perumāḷ*.) The meaning of the word is one with great power or simply prince. A poetic way of referring to the Lord is *emperumān* (my Lord). This corresponds to the Hewbrew Adonai (אֲדֹנָי).

This stanza reveals an insight into what bioogists call Darwinian evolution, for it lists the various forms of life: aquatic, avian, mammalian, etc, through which one goes before becoming a human. And we have the potential to go beyond. The poet speaks of inanimate stones as prior to life forms, and of immaterial beings also in the vast scheme of things.

The various incarnations mean life with all constraints and qualities, and at low levels before the awakening that puts us in awareness of the Supreme Principle that is at the root of it all. Indeed, the whole stanza is to remind us that there are a thousand different modes of existence, but all of these are incomplete and uncompleted until there comes about a spiritual realization. It is only when that arises that there is complete fulfillment.

The poet's weariness with life and eagerness to merge with the Divine reminds us of the first stanza of R. G. Wells' poem *Growing Older*:

A little more tired at the close of day,
A little more anxious to have our way,
A little less likely to scold and to blame,
A little more care for a brothers name;
And so we are nearing the journey's end,
Where time and eternity meet and blend.

7.2

மெய்யே உன் பொன் அடிகள் கண்டு
இன்று வீடு உற்றேன்

meyyē un pon aḍigaḷ kaṇḍu inḍṟu vīḍu uṭṟēn
In truth, seeing your golden feet, I have achieved emancipation today.

Word meanings

meyyē - in truth
un - your
pon - golden
aḍigaḷ - feet
kaṇḍu - having seen
inḍṟu - today
vīḍu - release, emancipation
uṭṟēn - I received

Explanatory Reflections

Consider a person who has been suffering from a series of ailments during many years. Finally, thanks to a medicine he receives unexpectedly, he is completely cured. What a great feeling of exhilaration that would be! Or again, imagine someone who had lost his sight or hearing, and then, all of a sudden, sight or sound come within the person's reach. This too would be a profoundly joyous experience.

Our poet exclaims that he has indeed had a very

similar experience, perhaps of a far greater order. For, he now feels he has been freed from the ancient ailment with which his soul had been afflicted: enchainment to *saṃsāra*: the birth-death cycle.

The word *mei* means truth in Tamil. Its opposite is *poi,* lie or falsehood. There is a wise saying in Tamil: *mei ninḍru vizukkiradu, poi koṅḍu porukkiradu*: Truth stands quietly, falsehood keeps blustering. That is to say, the wise keep silent while fools make all the noises.

Seeing the golden feet of the Lord means that he has recognized the true nature of physical existence. When the poet says he has been emancipated from the shackles of saṃsāra, he expresses the idea that those who have attained spiritual enlightenment begin to regard the world from very different perspectives, and are not affected by the trifles and trivialities that pester others.

The Latin poet Horace put it this way in his *Satires* (7):

> Who then is free? The wise man, who is lord over himself whom neither poverty, nor death, nor bonds affright, who bravely defies his passions, and scorns ambition, who in himself is a whole, smooth and rounded, so that nothing from outside can rest on the

> polished surface, or against whom Fortune in her onset is ever defeated.

The description of Horace's wise man is in many ways appropriate to the spiritually evolved person too, for such a person also defies passion, is also unaffected by poverty or death, scorns ambition, is not frightened by bonds. That is why the enlightened ones are said to have attained wisdom.

7.3

உய்ய என் உள்ளத்துள் ஓங்காரமாய் நின்ற

uyya en uḷḷattuḷ ōṅkāramāi ninḍṟa

That I may benefit, standing in my heart as the Om-syllable

Word meanings

uyya - to benefit from

en - my

uḷḷattuḷ - in heart

ōṅgkāramāi - as the sound of Om

ninḍṟa - which stood

Explanatory Reflections

The Sivapurāṇam begins with a mantra: *Namasivāya*. A mantra is a sacred verse or utterance. It may be a single syllable or several lines in length. Its important characteristic is that it is spiritually potent: it has the power to transform the one who utters it and others too.

Of the many mantras in Indic traditions, some are known as *bījāksharas* or seed-syllables. A *bījākshara* consists of only one syllable, and it must end in a nasal sound, called *anusvara* in Sanskrit. The best known and most universally chanted *bījākshara* mantra in the Hindu tradition is *aum*. This monosyllable is referred to as *aum-kāra*.

In the scriptural literature of Hinduism there are several interpretations of this mantra. The *Manḍukya Upanishad* expounds the meanings of aum. Its three components are said to reflect the three Vedas (*Rig, Sāma,* and *Yajur*), as also the triple principle of Creation (*Brahmā*), Sustenance (*Vishṇu*), and Dissolution (*Shiva*). According to a tāntric interpretation the coming together of the lips in the utterance of the *bhījākshara* is symbolic of the union of Shiva and Shakti which resulted in Cosmic Birth. This could be regarded symbolic of the idea that the Cosmic Creation emerged from the merger or synthesis of fundamental dichotomies. That is why the proper enunciation of this mantra is so significant.

One of the fundamental discoveries of twentieth century physics is that the physical universe is sustained such as it is because of certain fundamental imperceptible universal vibrations, known as vacuum fluctuations. Likewise, efforts to account for the existence of multiplicity in the theoretical model of the so-called string-theories envisions fundamental vibrations at the root of ultimate reality. It is remarkable that the notion of the *bījākshara* reflects a very similar insight: namely that there is a cosmic vibration undergirding the universe. The mantra *aum* is a sonic representation of that universe-sustaining principle.

Our poet says in this line that the *aum-kāra* is deeply engraved in his heart. The ultimately Hindu vision is expressed here.

7.4

மெய்யா விமலா விடைப்பாகா வேதங்கள்

meiyyā vimalā viḍaippāgā vēdaṅggaḷ

As truth, as purity, as the Bull, the Vedas

Word meanings

meiyyā - as truth

vimalā - as blemishless

viḍaippāgā - as bull/as difference

vēdaṅkaḷ - Vedas

Explanatory Reflections

In the Vedic tradition Divinity is Truth: *satyam*. This word is also related to the word for essence. The corresponding Tamil word is *mei*. The essence of something is called meipporuḷ. The poet says that the Supreme is the Truth, the essence of everything. God is the Ultimate Reality, the only truth there is. This view regards God, not in anthropomorphic terms, but as the quintessence of the experienced world, of all of Creation.

Another attribute of God is perfection. That which is perfect is also pure, without spot or blemish. That which is impure is called *malam*. One Sanskrit/Tamil word for purity is *vimalam*: the non-impure state. Correspondingly those who wish to experience the Divine must also have a pure state of mind: i.e. they must be devoid of impure thoughts.

When the Divine is pictured as Shiva, we also refer to some of Shiva's mythic characteristics. In the tradition, the bull is closely linked to Shiva. There are several reasons for this. One is that the bull is regarded as a very strong creature, and is symbolic of the virility associated with Lord Shiva. Shiva is therefore pictured as the lord of the bull. That is the reason why, for the worshippers of Siva, the bull is a very sacred animal. One will find in practically every Shiva temple, the bull known as *Nandin* (*Nandi* in Tamil). He is one of the two guardians of Lord Siva. Basava (12th century) the founder of a devout sect of Shaivas, the Liṅgāyats, is also known as *Vṟishaba* (Bull), because he is said to have been an incarnation of Nandi.

In the Saiva Siddhānta tradition Nandi is said to have been the guru of Tirumūlar, one of the foremost Saiva Siddhāntins and author of the massive work *Tirumandiram*: Sacred Chants.

Some have traced the worship of Nandin to the Indus Valley civilization. It may be mentioned in passing that the worship of the cow and bull is not unique to the Hindu tradition. Somewhat like Manu's injunction, there used to be a law in ancient Rome which regarded the killing of a bull as equivalent to the killing of a human being.

In classical Tamil (*kazagattamiz*), the word *viḍaippu* also means difference. So one might also interpret this to mean one who is manifest in different forms. The last word *vedangaḷ* in this line is to be connected with the next line.

7.5

ஐயா எனவோங்கி ஆழ்ந்து அகன்ற நுண்ணியனே

aiyā ena ōṅgi āzndu agaṇḍṟa nuṇṇiyanē

Elevated as Oh Lord (by the Vedas), deep, all-pervasive, Oh subtle one!

Word meanings

aiyā - O Lord
ena - thus
(v)ōṅgi - raising
āzndu - going deep
agandra - moved, spread
nuyṇṇiyanē - O subtle one!

Explanatory Reflections

The poet says that the Divine was proclaimed as the Lord by the Vedas. But the Divine rose much higher than the reach even of the Vedas. Divinity went very deep also, and spread all over.

What is one to make of the statement that the Vedas proclaim the Divine as the Lord. Perhaps the poet is reminding us that all the scriptures of the world personify the Divine as they sing hymns and pray and laud the Divine. But the Divine is way above what we can extol in words. Scriptures are like the sun in the verse below:

The rising sun to mortal right reveals

The earthly globe, but yet the stars conceals.
So may the sense discover natural things,
Divine above the reach of human wings.

If we try to picture the Divine in lofy thoughts, that too is not very successful because Divinity is too deep for our minds to grasp. It is like some precious stone at the bottom of the ocean, not within reach of even those who dive a hundred feet below the surface.

The Divine is all-pervasive, yet nowhere to be recognized with our normal modes of perception. The immanence of the Divine is referred to here. Immanence refers to the inner presence of God within ourselves, but also to the presence of God in all of creation. G. K. Chesterton ignored the second aspect when he wrote (*Orthodoxy*): "By insisting specially on the immanence of God we get introspection, self-isolation, quietism, social indifference..."

Like the ether of classical physics, the Divine pervades every nook and corner of space, for it is the Absolute. Like the ether again, it is hyperfine, too subtle to be spotted. What is conveyed here is that the Divine is not a tangible, substantial entity, a person like you and me, but is beyond space and time, beyond matter and energy, for that is what transcendence is. When Albert Einstein said *Raffiniert is der Herrgott* - Subtle is the Lord, he was unknowingly echoing this line of Sivapurāṇam.

8.1

வெய்யாய், தணியாய், இயமானனாம் விமலா

veiyyāi taṇiyāi iyamānanām vimalā
As harsh and mitigating, as Master,
the blemishless One

Word meanings

veyyāi - as a hot/harsh one
taṇiyāi - as mitigator, diminisher
iyamānanām - as the master
vimalā - as the blemishless, as the pure one

Explanatory Reflections

In life, we encounter pain and suffering. It would seem that God is not always merciful.. He is like the heat of the sun that is sometimes scorching. But it is good to remember that the pain and suffering that we experience and see have been caused by ourselves. In the *karma* framework, whatever we experience as unpleasant is the result of our own past actions. In so far as they are subject to the law of *karma* instituted by God, we may say that God is harsh. Stay for long in a tropical summer sun and you can get your skin burnt. Is that the fault of the sun or our own reckless behavior? Only in this sense is God harsh and hurtful.

On the other hand, it is good to recognize that

any lessening of the pain we experience must be a blessing from God, says the poet, for it is the Divine that mitigates the inevitable kārmic woes. Here is a beautiful and helpful idea. Rather than blame God for our troubles, we may be grateful that the misfortune was not as great as it could have been. This is what is meant by calling God a diminisher or mitigator. We are reminded that often we suffer less than how much we really deserve. We are reminded here of the line in the Wisdom of Solomon, "Mercy will soon pardon the meanest."

When the law of *karma* is in full swing, who is to alleviate the normal operation of a law? Only the Almighty can. In the Vedic framework, the *yajamāna* (Sanskrit) is the chief in a Vedic sacrifice who conducts the rituals as per the prescribed rules. By the use of this word *(iyamānanām)* here, the poet makes us picture all that is transpiring in the world as a cosmic drama of which Divinity is the Master of Ceremonies. God creates the show and handles it the way He chooses.

In the performance of that role, the Divine is without blemish, for the world functions in perfect accordance with the rules that have been set. The laws of nature can never be broken, except by the grace of the One who has created it all. So we can never dodge the consequences of our action: sooner or later, they will catch up with us. But now and again, we may be spared extreme pain because the Supreme is also one who alleviates pain: hence he is referred to as a mitigator.

8.2

பொய் ஆயின எல்லாம் போய் அகல வந்தருளி

poi āyina ellām pōi agala vandaruḷi

All untruth removed the grace that came

Word meanings

poi - a lie

āyina - what became

ellām - all, everything

pōi - having gone

agala - that it may move away

vandu - having come

aruḷi - having graced

Explanatory Reflections

The reference here is to the thesis in one school of Hindu metaphysics: That we live in a framework of errors, illusions, and confusions. All these may be described as lies that the world plays on us. However, this happens only at a certain level of experience.

For example, prior to an understanding that comes from detailed observational astronomy, one thought that the earth was at the center of the universe. But when we are awakened to a deeper level of comprehension we realize that this is not so. The geocentric view is a lie that Nature says, or rather our normal perceptual faculties tell us.

Many aspects of the phenomenal world are like this. Whether it is the rainbow or an oasis, or countless other things, first impressions often tend to be wrong. But it is only after acquiring true knowledge that we realize we were wrong in our assessment; that, in fact, we had been deluded.

The poet says that he has now recognized all those falsehoods which he had taken for the truth. How did the illusions melt away? It was because of the grace he had received. Spiritual realization may be interpreted as an awakening that occurs as a result of a blessing from the transcendent. It is only when one has received such grace that one is able to discriminate the essence from the fluff, the kernel from the chaff.

Such grace clears the mind by taking away the lies, the delusions to which we are normally subjected. This is what the poet is telling us here. We are reminded of Shankaracharya's aphorism, *brahma satyam, jagat mithya*: Brahman is Real, the World is a Lie, meaning that this experienced world is not to be confused with Ultimate Reality.

Recall Shakespeare's Antipholus of Syracuse in *The Comedy of Errors,* saying:

And here we wander in illusions;

Some blessed power deliver us from hence!

We will be able to recognize the illusions of the magician as no more than a trick only if and when the magician reveals to us the truth about the matter. Likewise, only those who, like the poet, have been privy to the esoteric truths, will be able to see the Truth.

8.3

மெய் ஞானம் ஆகி மிளிர்கின்ற மெய்ச் சுடரே

mei ñānamāgi miḷirginḍṟa meich chuḍarē

Oh brilliant one that is magnificent
as true wisdom

Word meanings

mei - truth

ñānam - wisdom

āgi - having become

miḷirgindra - (who is) becoming great, is shining

mei - truth

chuḍarē - oh brilliant one!

Explanatory Reflections

This is another line in the work which is addressed directly to the Divine. Here Divinity is pictured as the focus of all wisdom.

The word *mei* is interesting. As mentioned earlier. it means truth, and is the opposite of *poi* which means falsehood.

However, *mei* usually stands for higher truth. In this sense, *mei ñānam* is spiritual enlightenment. One who has attained it called a *meiñāni*. Likewise a scholar who is versed in the higher philosophies is sometimes called a *meikkaṇḍa-dēvar*. In fact, this is the name of a saintly personage who lived in the thirteenth century who is said to have seen the higher truth. His Siva nana Bodham is a sacred work in the Tamil Shaiva tradition.

The word *mei* also means the physical body. Thus a cloak is called a *meippāḍam*. A consonant is called *mei ezuttu*: body letter, and a vowel is *uyir ezuttu*: soul letter, since it gives life to the sound of a letter.

The possession of truth makes a person great. "Truth is precious and divine," said Samuel Butler. This is certainly true of higher or esoteric truths. The Divine, being pure Truth of the highest order, becomes great (*miḷargiṟār*). Like the sun, the Divine becomes brilliant (*chuḍar*). We could also take this to mean that those who have attained the highest level of enlightenment, the sages and ascetics of a tradition, shine in their spiritual luster, for a little of that divine effulgence has entered them.

We are reminded here of the lines of Thomas Campbell (*The Pleasures of Hope* -I):

> Truth shall restore the light by Nature given
> And, like Prometheus, bring the light of Heaven.

Transferring this divine quality to humans, we say that a person who has reached a state of wisdom in values and understanding has attained enlightenment. This is different from mere intelligence. A brilliant individual may not necessarily be an enlightened one.

8.4

எஞ்ஞானம் இல்லாதேன்

இன்பப் பெருமானே

eññānam illādēn inbapperumānē

(I am) without an iota of wisdom,

Oh loving Lord!

Word Meanings

eññānam - any wisdom

illādēn - I am without

inba - (of) bliss

perumānē - o Lord!

Explanatory Reflections

The world knows, as his contemporaries knew, that Māṇikkavāsakar was a man of no mean attainments. It was no secret that he possessed enormous spiritual wisdom. Then, we might wonder, why does he describe himself as a poor soul who is devoid of any wisdom?

One of the traditional modes of approaching the Almighty in any religious tradition, and certainly in the Hindu tradition, is to surrender oneself to God by falling prostrate at the feet of the Lord. This is known as *charaṇāgati*. It is an expression of utter humility in the face of God. It is an explicit recognition that ultimately it is in God that one takes refuge from the pains and sufferings, perplexities and confusions of life.

After referring to the Divine as the pinnacle of all wisdom, the poet states that he himself has absolutely no wisdom. A hundred billion is not a small number, but compared to infinity, it is like zero.

Humility is not self-effacement or self-demeaning, but a contextual recognition of one's limitations. The school teacher need not proclaim her limited knowledge to her pupils, but when a person of modest learning is in the presence of a great scholar of world renown, it is appropriate that one recognizes one's smallness in that context. What is relevant is not the knowledge and wisdom per se, nor where it stands with respect to other people one may came across, but how one estimates it with reference to the Divine.

The saying of the poetess Auvaiyār to the effect that what has been learned is but like a handful of mud compared to cosmic dimensions of what has not been learned, is an acknowledgment of finiteness in the face of infinity. That is what humility is al labout.

Swami Sivananda once said, "Humility is not cowardice. Meekness is not weakness. Humility and meekness are indeed spiritual powers." Henry

Thoreau wrote in his *Walden* that "humility, like darkness, reveals the heavenly lights." That is what is illustrated here. By declaring his own insignificance in the face of the grand Almighty, the poet reveals the heavenly light that is within him.

Note also that the poet refers to the Divine as the Lord of bliss, for experience of the divine transcends all joys: it is bliss supreme. Whereas limited and confused visions of God make the Divine a source of fear, terror, and punishment, in awakened religious perspectives God is a source of love, joy, and ecstasy.

8.5

அஞ்ஞானம் தன்னை அகல்விக்கும் நல் அறிவே

añňānan tannai agalvikkum nal arivē

Oh benign wisdom that removes ignorance

Word Meanings

añňānam - ignorance, lack of wisdom

tannai - it (accusative)

agalvikkum - makes leave, move away from,

nalla - good

arivē - oh sense!

Explanatory Reflections

Since ancient times, poets and thinkers have reflected on the ignorance that misguides us all. The Latin poet Ovid exclaimed:

Pro superi! Quantum mortalia pectoral cæcæ!

O Gods! How much darkness there is in mortal's minds!

Shakespeare put it pithily thus: "There is no darkness but ignorance."

Since ignorance is darkness, we look upon knowledge as light. Where the light of knowledge dawns the darkness of ignorance disappears.

We may note in passing the sound-resemblance between *añňānam* and ignorance, one derived from the Sanskrit *jnāna*: knowledge, and the other from the Greek *gnosis*: (spiritual) knowledge.

Both knowledge and ignorance can be at two levels. One is about worldly matters, about things and places and the scientific nature of things. This knowledge enables us to do well in the world, and manipulate it also. Ignorance of this makes us science-illiterate and inadequate in many contexts.

The other dimension of knowledge and ignorance is about the true nature of existence and of ultimate reality. It is of this that our poet is speaking here. It is this knowledge that enables us to develop a perspective on things as we go through life. It is the source of love and compassion, of caring and humility. The absence of this kind of knowledge is what is meant by *aññānam*. When this knowledge comes to us, our tendencies for pettiness and unkindness, for jealousy and envy, for anger and pride and such melt away; and our capacity for doing good and being good is enhanced. That is why it says in the Book of Job: "The price of wisdom is above rubies."

The eighteenth century French philosopher Antoine Bret wrote with a touch of sarcasm: *Le* premier soupir *de l'amour est le dernier de la sagesse.* the first sigh of love is the last sigh of wisdom. He was referring to romantic man-woman love. On the other hand, the highest wisdom is when one is capable of love towards all creatures. Wisdom is that kind of knowledge, which prompts us to not only think of God and the good, but also act with love and kindness, caring and compassion. It is easy to preach these things and repeat the mantras we have learned. What really matters is how we apply such values in the course of our everyday life. Removal of ignorance involves the erasing of egocentric behavior.

9.1

ஆக்கம் அளவு இறுதி இல்லாய்,

அனைத்து உலகும்

ākkam aḷavu iṟudi illāi anaittulagum

You are without transformation, measure. The whole world

Word Meanings

ākkam - growth, transformation

aḷavu - measure

iṟudi - end

illāi - you are without

anaitta - all

ulagum - the world

Explanatory Reflections

An interesting feature of all things of finite existence is that they don't maintain the same size for all times. Indeed, many of them grow in size. Whether rivers or mountains, they gradually become larger with time, and this is of course true of all living entities: plants and trees, animals and humans. Growth also implies transformation. Thinkers have recognized since ancient times that everything changes. Ovid wrote in his *Metamorphoses*:

> All things change, nothing is extinguished. . . . There is nothing in the

> whole world which is permanent. Everything flows onward; all things are brought into being with a changing nature; the ages themselves glide by in constant movement.

Growth implies size, and size implies measurement. Things grow from small to big, from tiny to huge. Such measure is also a feature of finite things. One cannot speak of the size of the infinite, for the infinite is, by definition, beyond all measure. That is why the poet refers to the Divine as beyond measure.

There is a price for change and measure. Everything that changes comes to an end sooner or later. In the very process of change a person or thing loses a little of the original identity, in the long run the entire entity vanishes. Decay and end are inevitable concomitants of all that changes.

The one that does not change is the Infinite. The Divine is, by definition, that which remains for ever the same. There is no transformation, no growth or end here.

This line ends with the word *world*, which is the beginning of the next few lines wherein the poet refers to the role of the Divine in this world, as also its relationship to life and existence, as envisaged in

MANIKKAVASAKAR'S SIVAPURANAM

Saiva Siddhāntam.

9.2

ஆக்குவாய் காப்பாய் அழிப்பாய் அருள் தருவாய்

ākkuvāi kāppāi azippāi aruḷ taruvāi

You create, protect, destroy, and give grace!

Word Meanings

ākkuvāi - you make/create

kāppāi - you protect

azippāi - you destroy

aruḷ - grace

taruvāi - you give

Explanatory Notes

In the traditional framework, the creation, sustenance, and dissolution of the universe is attributed to a triple principle: Brahmā creates, Vishṇu sustains, and Shiva destroys. In the framework of Saiva Siddhāntam, all these are attributed to Sivan. Thus it is one and the same Divinity that creates the entire cosmos that protects it, and finally destroys it all.

First there must be a universe, or else, there is only void. So the first thing that Divinity does is to create the world. Every religious tradition attributes the creation of the world to an almighty transcendent entity. In the Judeo-Christian *Book of*

Genesis we read that it was God who created the world of light and life. Then there is God the sustainer. In the Psalms of the Old Testament we read:

> He maketh me to lie down in the green pastures,
> He leadeth me beside the still waters.
> He restoreth my soul; he leadeth me in the paths
> of righteousness for his name's sake.

But ultimately, all created things must come to an end. That too is the work of the Divine. Sooner or later there comes a time for every creature and for every thing in the universe to decay and die. This is an evitable aspect of every created entity. There is something sad and sinister in the thought of the complete dissolution of everything in the universe, including our own individual consciousness. But there is a saving grace in all of this. For, says the poet, the Divine also gives us grace (*aruḷ*). That grace compensates for all the gloom and doom of eventual death. Divine grace is not simply generous care while we are here below, but a promise for the hereafter.

In most religious traditions those who have received grace are expected to merge with the

Divine, or enter the portals of heaven, whatever the metaphor, when all is said and done. In this line the poet adds a fourth quality of the Divine, the bestowing of grace. Note that the other three: creation, sustenance, and dissolution, can be for any entity, animate or inanimate. But grace is meaningful only to a fully conscious being: to human beings. In ither words, grace, and thus God, become relevant only in the context of humanity. Without us, this will be a routine, mechanical, mindless world, without love or joy, without blessing or grace.

9.3

போக்குவாய் என்னைப் புகுவிப்பாய் நின் தொழும்பின்

pōkkuvāi ennai puguvippāi nin tozumbin

You have sent me here to make me part of those who serve you

Word Meanings

pōkkuvāi - you make go

ennai - me

puguvippāi - you make me a part

nin - your

tozumbin - in the service

Explanatory Reflections

The world was created by the Divine. We are not only creatures in it, but we are meant to serve the Creator. The poet says that the Divine principle has sent us here and is enabling us to be part of the multitude that act as instruments in so many ways.

There is an allusion here to what is known in the framework of Saivasiddāntam as *aintozil* the five functions of the Divine. These are:

shirushṭi: creation. Corresponding to this divine action, creatures also reproduce, doing Divinity's work. The process of creating progeny is referred to as an imitation, as it were, of what the Divine had done for the whole world.

stiti: maintenance of the created world. Creatures also serve to maintain in their own ways the world and other creatures around them. We note again the insightful parallel between our efforts to preserve things in the world, and the divine action by which the world is sustained.

chaṅgāral: destruction. It is part of divine action to bring to a close everything. In our own ways, we also engage in some destruction. Here again, it is not just Divinity that dissolves and destroys. We humans do this also. Thus, all the triple roles of God are repeated, albeit at much more modest levels, by humans also. This reflects the Hindu view that there is a little of the Divine in each of us.

tirōbavam: This is a feature of Divinity by which the Divine is hidden from us. One may say that the purpose of this is to induce us to search for it. In other words, it is the hidden nature of the Divine that provokes the quest. Another interpretation could be that here the poet is referring to the view in the mystical tradition that God and knowledge about God belong to the realm of the occult.

The word *anukkiragam* means grace or blessing that the Divine bestows us. The poet says that it is because of that grace that we have been given this opportunity to serve the Divine in our different ways. The recognition that service is an aspect of true spirituality needs to be emphasized, for mere individual mystical embrace of the transcendence serves no purpose at all for humanity at large.

9.4

நாற்றத்தின் நேரியாய், சேயோய், நணியானே

nāṯṟattin nēriyāi cēyāi naṇiyānē

Subtler than fragrance, Who is far and near!

Word Meanings

nāṯṟattin - more than fragrance

nēriyāi - being subtle

cēyāi - being distant

naṇiyānē - oh near one!

Explanatory Reflections

Poets are known for their similes. It is sometimes said that the originality of the similes is a reflection of one's poetic and writing abilities. The poet Wordsworth wrote:

Oft on the dappled turf at ease
I sit and play with similes,
Loose type of things in all degrees.

Tamil poets are reputed for their imaginative similes. The poet Kamban's work is stunning in its ample and telling use of these.

Here the poet uses a peculiar kind of simile in that he compares a quality rather than a thing. It is not an image but a concept that he invokes. He wants to convey the subtlety of the Divine. For this he takes our mind to the fragrance of flowers.

Fragrance is not something we see or touch or can hold. Yet its presence can be felt, and often we know that it is permeating the air around us.

By this simile, the poet says that the subtlety of the Divine exceeds even the subtlety of fragrance, and is just as enjoyable.

Then comes the idea that God is both far and near. The word *naṇiyān* comes from *naṇimai* which means proximity, nearness. This can be interpreted in two ways. First, God is one of the most elusive entities in the universe, and seems very distant, unapproachable, and even unimaginable. At the same time, those who have had any mystical experience at all, or a profound feeling of connectedness with the Whole, as during a prayer or meditation, have felt deep in their hearts that God is somehow very, very close to them. God seems to be up there in the heavens, but is actually within us.

In other words, Divinity is not something to be comprehended in terms of logical categories. No thing or person can be both distant and near, but God can, and God is.

Here we are also reminded of the Chinese proverb which says: "Make happy those who are near, and those who are far will come." Likewise, if we pay adequate attention to the God within and the God in our immediate vicinity, the distant God will come to us.

9.5

மாற்றம் மனம் கழிய நின்ற மறையோனே

māṯṟam manam kaziya ninḍṟa maṟaiyōnē

You, Who is in wisdom, transcending word and mind

Word Meanings

māṯṟam - word

manam - mind

kaziya - cutting off

ninḍṟa - having stood

maṟaiyōnē - O, One of esoteric word!

Explanatory Reflections

In many spiritual traditions, there is the notion of an all-pervading reason behind the phenomenal world. This is expressed as Logos (the Greek for word) in the Christian tradition. Logos is sacred and is symbolic of the Divine. The idea is there in Hellenic, Persian, and Hebraic traditions as well. The Tirukkuuṟaḷ invokes God as the wielder of all letters in the world.

The word is associated with the mind. Every word, uttered or written, comes from the mind. With all its marvelous capacities the mind is also limited. Thus *māṯṟam* and *manam* (Word and Mind) cover the entire world of ideas and experience. The poet addresses the Divine as one Who has gone beyond word and mind, for Divinity is in the transcendent realm which is not subject to the finite and the ephemeral, such as the entities of our world are. But what is that transcendent world, and what is its nature? Answers to such questions constitute occult knowledge.

We may also interpret this line as saying that when we go beyond the words of everyday existence, and the mind that is tied to these, we reach the realm of occult wisdom. That is why *mantras* are more than what they literally mean. In Tamil, the word *maṟaippadu* means to hide. Therefore the word *maṟai* refers to hidden (i.e. esoteric) knowledge which is embodied in sacred writings. The four Vedas are known as *nānmaṟai* in Tamil. Given that the Divine is the source of Vedic wisdom, it is addressed here as *maṟaiyōn*. It may be pointed out that technically this word also refers to Brahmā. On the other hand, *maṟaittalaivi* is a name for Lakshmi. Thus, in the Tamil language, the word *maṟai*, meaning that which is esoteric, connects the triple principle in the Hindu framework: Brahmā, Vishṇu (whose consort is Lakshmi), and Shiva (whom the poet invokes through this word here).

Recall the words of Hamlet's father in the Shakespearean play: "My words fly up, my thoughts remain below: Words without thoughts never to heaven go." The king realizes that though his words utter prayer, his thoughts are yet petty, since the reason for the prayer is not genuine repentance but the hope that he would be spared from being discovered. All thoughts and words, good and bad, belong to our ephemeral world. But God is transcends all this.

10.1

கறந்த பால் கன்னலொடு நெய்கலந்தாற் போல

karanda pāl kannaloḍu nei kalandāṟ pōla

As fresh milk is like sugar-candy and ghee

Word Meanings

kaṟanda - extracted

pāl - milk

kannaloḍu - with sugar cane

nei - clarified butter (ghee)

kalandāl - if mixed

pōla - like

Explanatory Reflections

Here is the beginning of another simile. The poet is referring to a most delicious concoction: a potion that is made up of fresh milk, the juice of sugar cane, and clarified butter. Or perhaps, he is simply describing the intrinsic taste of milk as of a combination of the sweetness of candy added to the fatness of butter.

Milk is invoked as a basic sustenance of life. In response to the first shrieks after birth, the new-born is fed mother's milk. Milk keeps us alive and kicking during the early formative stages of our lives. So the idea of milk is appropriately linked to that of the Divine who cares for us all through our existence.

Next there is sweetness. To taste the sweet is one of the supreme satisfactions of life. Yet, with all the power that words possess, we can never convey the meaning of sweetness to one that has never experienced it. As Dante wrote in another context:

Mind cannot follow it, nor words express
Her infinite sweetness.

Then comes the fatness of butter which expresses substance. We are still in the mortal frame. So the experience of sweetness, whether of lingual satisfaction or divine ecstasy, needs to have a substance-basis, and that is what butter (ghee) represents.

We nourish our bodies with milk, which tastes like sugar mingled with the fatness of butter. Likewise, we must nourish our souls by extracting the spiritual essence that comes from an awareness of the Divine. We are reminded of the magical alchemy that is the experience of body (fat) spirit (milk), and experience (sweetness). We may recall here of the poet Coleridge's lines:

For he on honey-dew hath fed,
And drunk the milk of Paradise.

10.2

சிறந்தடியார் சிந்தனையுள் தேனூறி நின்று

chiṟandaḍiyār chindanaiyuḷ tēn ūṟi ninḍṟu

In the minds of great devotees You stood as flowing honey

Word Meanings

chiṟandu - great, excellent

aḍiyār - devotees

chindaiyuḷ - in the minds of

tēn - honey

ūṟi - flowing

ninḍṟu - staying

Explanatory Reflections

Where does the Divine reside, and in what way? The poet answers these questions by saying that Divinity is present in the minds of those whose thoughts are always in the Divine. Then one may ask: Does this mean that the Divine is a purely subjective experience? That is certainly not the implication here. The significance of this statement is that in the world of humans here on earth, the Divine is reflected in all its splendor in the consciousness of a few. These are the glorious devotees (*chiṟandaḍiyār*) of the Divine.

In Tamil, the word *chiṟandar* may also refer to the rich and the famous, and *tuṟanḍōr* means those who have renounced the world: ascetics. The word *aḍiyār* literally means those who are at the feet of someone: i.e. slaves. metaphorically, in spiritual literature the word *slave* is used for the most genuine devotees of a particular manifestation of the Divine. Thus *Sivanaḍiyār* refers to a devotee of Lord Shiva.

It is interesting that the poet does not call the devotees of the Divine *tuṟandaḍiyār*: ascetic devotees, but *chiṟandaḍiyar*: rich and renowned devotees. The implication is that the exceptional among those who have acquired this divine consciousness are truly rich in what they experience, and they also become renowned in the world. In other words, here the rich and the famous does not refer to celebrities and jet-setters, as it does in our own times. How the values in a culture can change!

At the highest level the devotee of God gives himself up to the Divine. In the human world, slave is a bad word because a slave is bought and sold and owned and exploited by other men. In the bhakti tradition, to become a slave (*dāsan, aDimai*) of God is the highest level of spiritual fulfillment. That is why we have names like Rāmdās, Bhagvāndās, etc. In the Islamic tradition too the name Abdullah (*abd* or slave + Allah or God) simply means servant of God. The *bhakta* says that everything that one has belongs to the Almighty, including one's body and soul. This corresponds to what is known in Vaishṅavism as *prapatti.* This concept of complete surrender to the Divine, is one of the things that Shaivas and VaishNavas have in common.

We may note in passing that in ancient Babylonian myths, humans were created literally as slaves to serve the gods Enki and Namma.

The poet goes on to say that the nectar of the Divine is flowing in their souls, as it were, for what they experience is an ineffable sweetness, that is to say an ecstasy that has no parallel in the world of ordinary experience. Symbols and aspects of Divinity may be seen in temples and prayer books, in worship services and hymns, but the essence of the Divine can only be tasted by those who have truly had the grace.

Neale D. Walsch said, in his *Conversations With God (III)* that "God is in sadness and laughter, in the bitter and the sweet." Our poet says that even in sadness and what is bitter, the sweetness of God can be felt by those who have experienced the Divine.

MANIKKAVASAKAR'S SIVAPURANAM

10.3

பிறந்த பிறப்பு அறுக்கும் எங்கள் பெருமான்

piṟanda piṟappu aṟukkum eṅgaḷ peṟumān

Our Lord Who cuts off the (future) births of the born ones

Word Meanings

piṟanda - that are born

piṟappu - birth

aṟukkum - that which cuts

eṅgaḷ - our

perumān - Lord

Explanatory Reflections

In the Hindu framework of birth and re-birth, the impact-causing actions (*karma*) during the lifetime of an individual has consequences on the doer. In principle, it is impossible to evade these consequences. That, in fact, is why one is re-born. In the Abrahamic religious framework, a person remains for eons after death until the Day of Judgment, then to be appropriately rewarded or punished.

In the Hindu view there is no easy escape from this cycle. Moreover, there is no life on earth that is without woe. Every person, no matter how rich and healthy at one time, no matter how fortunate in kith and kin and mind, will have to experience pain and suffering, and eventual death through sickness, accident, or old age, leaving behind a host of wailing family and friends.

So the goal of life is to act in ways that would minimize the inevitable pain and suffering in the next birth, or better still, avoid re-birth altogether. This can be achieved either by exceptional good conduct, severance of attachment, and ascetic attachment to God; or by a special boon from the Almighty that comes as grace. Yes, everyone can pray and plead for this, even as everyone may buy a lottery ticket. But, as with lottery, not everyone is a winner in this matter.

The Divine is the only one that has the power to cut off this chain of birth and death, release the soul from this recurring torment, and draw it back into the cosmic consciousness from which it arose in the first place. This is equivalent to the belief in other traditions that God is our only savior.

The effort and eagerness to escape from the birth-death-birth cycle, as well as devotion to God to achieve it, are frequent themes in the thoughts of many spiritually inclined people and in the writings of thinkers, writers, and sages.

10.4

நிறங்கள் ஓர் ஐந்து உடையாய், விண்ணோர்கள் ஏத்த

niṟaṅgaḷ ōr aindhu uḍaiyāy, viṇṇōrgal ētta

United in the five colors, lauded by celestials

Word Meanings

niṟaṅgaḷ - colors

ōr - one

aindu - five

uḍaiyāi - you have

viṇṇōrgaḷ - celestial beings

ētta - lauded

Explanatory Reflections

There are some esoteric and purāṅic allusions in this line. In one puraṇic vision Lord Shiva has five faces. These are known as *isāna*: the One of the north-east; *tatpurusha*: that Purusha; *akōram*: the Fierce One - of the south; *vāmanam*: the Dwarf; and *satyōjātam*: existence by Truth. Although in the Sanskritic tradition all the avatārās are of Vishṇu, according to *Chatur-agarāti,* a classic Tamil dictionary, Vāmana avatara was a Shiva incarnation.

In the framework of Saivasiddhānta, each of the letters of the panchākshara refers to one of the five faces of Siva, and is associated with a different color. Specifically, *na,* denoting *ānam,* is of golden color.

Denoting *tatpurushan* is *ma,* and it is white. The letter *si* stands for *agōram,* and is associated with red. The letter *vā;* denotes vāmanam and is black. Finally *ya* denotes satyōjātam and has the color gray.

The sacred number five associated with Shiva are said the symbolize the five primordial elements of earth water, air, fire, and ether, the five senses (sight, smell, taste, audition, and touch) and their corresponding perceptual organs.

It may be recalled in passing the number five is also sacred in Chinese thought and in some Buddhist traditions as well.

In all religious traditions, a powerful mode of experiencing the Divine is by paying homage to the Almighty. And this is done by singing praises of God's many attributes. That is why there are so many hymns and chants in all religious frameworks.

The poet says in this line that heavenly beings sing the praises of the Lord, reminding us of a Christmas carol where it says "Heaven and angels sing" when they hear about the birth of Christ. Indeed, in the religious vision, there is a world beyond the physical-phenomenal. This is the realm of supernatural beings, of *viṇṇōrgaḷ* as it says here. They live in perpetual joy in the presence of the

Almighty, and they sing for ever God's glory.

10.5

மறைந்திருந்தாய், எம்பெருமான்

maṟaindirundāi enperumān

You were hidden oh my Lord

Word Meanings

maṟaindu - hidden

irundāi - you were

en - my

perumān - lord

Explanatory Reflections

In this line the poet states that the esoteric aspects of the Divine remain hidden to one and all, even to the celestials. But he himself is now aware of them, which is why he says you *were* hidden, and not you *are* hidden. Those aspects refer to the ninety six essences (qualities) of the physical universe, known as *tattuvaṅgaḷ* (*tattvas*) in the framework of Saiva Siddhānta. According to the Varāhōpanishad, all these *tattvas* are below the *saguna brahman*. They consist of:

Five *būdaṅgal* or elements; five *poṟigaḷ* or sense organs; five *pulaṅgaḷ,* objects of the senses; five *karmēndiriyaṅgaḷ*: organs of action; five *ñānēndiriyaṅgaḷ*: organs of perception; four *andakkaraṅgaḷ*: intellectual faculties; one *aṟivu*: intelligence; ten *nāḍigaḷ*: arteries; ten *vāyukaḷ*: vital airs; five *āsayaṅgaḷ*: receptacles for the humors; five *kōsaṅgaḷ*: sheathes of the soul; three *manḍalaṅgaḷ*: the three regions of the body which are under the influence of the sun, the moon, and fire; three *malaṅgaḷ:* moral evils; three *dōshaṅgaḷ*: three humors; three *ēshaṅgaḷ*: principal desires; three *guṇaṅgal*: three fundamental qualities; eight *vigāraṅgaḷ*: dominant passions; two *vinaigaḷ,* vestiges of moral behavior; and five *avattaigaḷ*: states of the soul.

The listing reads like the Periodic Table of modern chemistry. To those unfamiliar with Hindu philosophical systems all this may be daunting. The spiritual framework of every school in Hindu philosophy includes extensive and complex categories in terms of which the mystery of existence and consciousness is understood. In the Sāmkhya system, the physical universe is seen in terms of twenty-four *tattvas* plus the *purusha.* The great sages and poets of the tradition refer to these directly or indirectly in their works.

11.1

வல்வினையேன் தன்னை மறைந்திட மூடிய மாய இருளை

valvinaiyēn tannai maṟaindiḍa mūḍiya māya iruḷai
Out of potent evil deeds one's true self closed, the darkness of illusion

Word Meanings

val - powerful

vinaiyēn - out of evil acts

tannai - oneself

maṟaindiḍa - so as to hide

mūḍiya - which was covered

māya - illusory

iṟuḷai - darkness (acc. case)

Explanatory Reflections

All our current experiences are essentially consequences of our *karma* in previous births. Most of those kārmic actions are of a negative kind, which is why every human life is wrought with pain and suffering. Moreover, the evil acts also cover our true self. That is to say, we are unable to see through the true nature of what we are.

What this means is that we are under a grand illusion as we walk through the journey of life. This grand illusion is equivalent to being in complete darkness, for we are indeed in the dark about the true nature of reality. This darkness of illusion is what the Hindu sages called *māyā*.

In this line the poet says that *māyā* arises from evil deeds; more exactly, spiritual darkness arises from evil deeds. This suggests that bad *karma* not only leads to pain and suffering and other unpleasantnesses in life, but also makes us spiritually blind. This is offered as an explanation for why some people seem to be perpetually insensitive to whatever is spiritual. Their insensitivity bars them from experiencing the true ecstasy that comes from a little bit of the Divine. It is the opposite of the statement that ignorance is bliss. It is somewhat like the fact that the inability to imagine things stands in the way of enjoying the delights of poetry, art, and grand literature. Here, we are reminded that ignorance is pain, that ignorance is ignorance of bliss.

The Buddha had said that the root cause of suffering was attachment and desire. Indeed these also result in the veil of ignorance that blind us from grasping the truc nature of the self, which is what spiritual enlightenment is all about. Every sinful thought, unpleasant word, and hurtful act reflects our baser nature. They hide what our true nature is:

for at the core of each of us there is a little of the Divine, covered and hidden. Only those who cleanse themselves of such accumulations, only the pure of heart will be able to realize the Self. One way of interpreting this line could be that that our own intrinsic goodness is a best kept secret from ourselves. In other words, we are often unaware of all the goodness and the positive things we are capable of.

As it says in the Bible (Matthew 5.8): "Blessed are the pure in heart, for they will see God."

11.2

அறம்பாவம் என்னும் அரும் கயிற்றால் கட்டி

aṟam pāvam ennum arum kayiṭṟāl kaṭṭi

Bound with the rare rope of sin and merit

Word Meanings

aṟam - righteousness

pāvam - sin

ennum - thus called

arum - rare

kayiṭṟāl - with the rope

kaṭṭi - bound

Explanatory Reflections

One might think that we will attain spiritual liberation by being good and doing only righteous acts. Not so, says the poet. Good *karma* also needs to be rewarded, and for this too one must take another birth. In other words, even meritorious actions will not liberate us from rebirth. For evil deeds one must return, there is no escape from that.

Thus, both good and bad behavior act as a strange kind of rope, one contributing to a golden strand and the other to a base one. This rope binds us to the perpetual cycle of birth and death. Perhaps this is what ensures the perpetuation of the species. From a theoretical point of view, if everyone escaped rebirth, all living people will become childless, for there will be no soul to return to earth.

This is an important matter to consider in this framework. It says, contrary to conventional wisdom, that while being good in one's life will lead to some pleasant experiences in the next birth, it is not going to release us from the suffering inherent in being born in mortal flesh. We are condemned to the birth-death cycle, no matter what: a no-win situation.

The point is, spiritual liberation is to be distinguished from receiving rewards in life. In the Hindu framework the goal of life should be to do whatever is necessary for attaining *mōksha*(*m*) which is complete liberation from the birth-death-rebirth cycle. There is a German saying that:

Leben ist gut, sterben is besser, nicht geboren ist am besten.

To live is good, to die is better, not to be born is the best of all.

Cute as this may sound, it really doesn't mean much. What can *not to be born* really signify? Does it make sense to say that the void is better off than the atoms it holds? There is no meaning to the statement that it is best not to be born. However, not to be born *again* means something. It means that that the individual soul has finally merged with the Supreme. It means that it is far better not to have another serving of a dish which, with all its deliciousness, will still cause us stomach ache in the end. We don't want to repeat an experience that is not without blemish.

One should rather say:

Leben ist gut, sterben ist nicht, aber nicht widergeboren ist am besten.

To live is good, to die is not, but not to be re-born is the best.

11.3

புறம்தோல் பார்த்து எங்கும் புழு அழுக்கு மூடி

puṟam tōl pārttu eṅgum puzu azukku mūḍi

Seeing the outer skin, the filth and worms being covered

Word Meanings

puṟam - external

tōl - skin

pārttu - having seen

eṅgum - everywhere

puzu - worms

azukku - dirt/filth

mūḍi - closing

Explanatory Reflections

We have a spiritual as well as a physical dimension. The spiritual draws us to the Divine. The physical keeps of chained to the worldly. The contrast between the two needs to be clearly understood. Without that understanding we are apt to remain in the dark for ever. Thomas Merton put it this way (*A Life in Letters*): "We stumble and fall constantly even when we are most enlightened. But when we are in true spiritual darkness, we do not even know that we have fallen." That is what our poet is reminding us of in this line.

In his *Biography of Saints,* Swami Sivananda mentions an anecdote in which the great sage-poet Tulsi Das once went to see his wife Ratnavali when she had gone to visit her parents for a few days, because he could not bear her absence. When his wife saw him come, hankering for her, she told him, "My body is but a network of flesh and bones. If you would develop for Lord Rama even half the love that you have for my filthy body, you would certainly cross the ocean of *Saṃsāra* and attain immortality and eternal bliss"

. We are reminded of what it says in the New Testament (Matthew 23:27): "Woe to you .... you hypocrites! You are like whitewashed tombs, which look beautiful on the outside but on the inside are full of dead men's bones and everything unclean."

Many thinkers have spoken of the crass aspect of the body. Shakespeare wrote, "What is thy body but a swallowing grave?" The Bible speaks of "our vile body." The Greek thinker Palladas wrote, "The body is an affliction of the soul. It is hell, fate, a burden, a necessity, a strong chain, and a tormenting punishment."

Thus we note that in most spiritual traditions there is this contempt for the physical body which man often finds difficult to resist in its attractive external features. Hence the despising of woman as the temptress in many religious traditions.

So it is that here our poet reminds us that beneath all the charm and beauty, the attractiveness and the voluptuousness, there is but flesh and bones and intestines filled with food digested and undigested, wherein thrive some lowly worms. Such is the true nature of our beautiful physical body. All its grossness is neatly hidden and covered by the external envelop of the skin. In due course even that withers and wrinkles. Yet, we are so attached to our own bodies. It is this unpleasant fact that we are prompted to reflect upon when we read this line.

In this context, it is not realized that such temptation is a biological evolutionary device to perpetuate the species.

MANIKKAVASAKAR'S SIVAPURANAM

11.4

மலம் சோரும் ஒன்பது வாயில் குடிலை

malam chōrum onpadu vāyil kuḍilai

Impurity flows through the nine doors of the hut

Word Meanings

malam - impurity

cōrum - will flow

onpadu - nine

vāyil - through the opening

kuḍilai - in the hut

Explanatory Reflections

This is a continuation of the lament on the gross physical body. The male body is described here as a modest dwelling with seven apertures: two of the eyes, two of the ears, two of the nostrils, one of the mouth, plus the urethra and the anal aperture. [In this framework, the female body is said to have three extra apertures, two nipples and one vaginal opening.]

Aside from being an observation on human anatomy, this has some esoteric significance in yogic and *tāntric* practice. Impurities flow through these openings in the everyday functioning of the body. Ordinarily we regard this as normal physiological processes. But in the spiritual tradition, one attaches esoteric significance to these.

The poet Walt Whitman wrote in his *Leaves of Grass,* "If anything is sacred, the human body is sacred." It is sacred, not only because it enshrines one of the most evolved entities in the universe, namely consciousness, but also because it is the seat of all spiritual experiences, one might argue. This view is certainly valid from physical and analytical perspectives on the human condition.

The tenet in the worldview presented in this line of the Sivapurāṇam is that discharges through the nine gates (*navdvāra*) of the body adversely affect the inner functioning. The gates are primarily for the ejection of bodily impurities. That also weakens our spiritual energies. This is the basis of this idea.

This is also the reason why complex yogic postures are recommended by which these apertures are sealed. This involves the use of eight fingers. The two thumbs close the holes in the ear, the index fingers close the eyes, the middle fingers close the nostrils, and the ring fingers are used to hold in tight contact the upper and the lower lips. The heels press on the perineum to close the urethra, and one contracts the anus. This is known as *shanmukhi*. The *jyoti mudra* is also a yogic mode for accomplishing this.

This is one reason why nine is a sacred number

in esoteric traditions. There are nine planets in traditional astrology, nine gems (*ratnas*), nine moods (*bhāvas*), Shankaracharya points out in *Soundarya Lahiri*, "The four Shiva chakras and five Shakti chakras create the nine *mūla*-prakritis or basic manifestations, because they represent the source substance of the whole cosmos". As the human body is taken as a microcosm which reflects the macrocosm, the nine-fold division is reflected there as nine apertures.

In this line the poet implicitly refers to this yogic thesis. In the works of great writers and poets there are always allusions to ideas and worldviews of the culture to which they belong.

11.5

மலங்கப் புலன் ஐந்தும் வஞ்சனையைச் செய்ய

malaṅgap pulan aindum vañchanai cheiyya

The sensory faculties confuse and deceive

Word Meanings

malaṅga - to confuse

pulan - faculties of perception

aindum - all the five

vañchanai - deceit

cheiyya - to do

Explanatory Reflections

The sun seems to rise in the east and set in the west. The rainbow is like a colorful arc spanning the sky. We sometimes feel we are hearing a ghost in the dark when it may be only an unusual rustling of leaves. Keep one hand in hot water and another in cold water for sometime, and then touch an object with both hands. The two hands will feel differently. These are all examples of false impressions of what is actually the case, illusions caused by our sensory faculties.

Classical Hindu philosophers wrote a good deal about the nature and reliability of our perceptual faculties. They quickly realized that the knowledge that we get via our *indriyas* (sensory faculties) is not always reliable. Though they also investigated and offered theories as to how exactly we perceive, they did not always concur. Thus, for example, the Sāmkhya view on the matter is different from the Nyāya view.

In this line the poet simply says that our senses confuse and deceive us about the nature of reality. This is a profound observation. Einstein is said to have observed that "reality is merely an illusion, albeit a very persistent one."

But why are illusions created?, one might wonder. Is it because, as T. S. Eliot observed, "humankind cannot bear very much reality?" Or is it because, as Sigmond Freud suggested, "illusions commend themselves to us because they save us pain and allow us to enjoy pleasure instead. We must therefore accept it without complaint when they sometimes collide with a bit of reality against which they are dashed to pieces." We do not know for sure.

Whatever the cause, when this realization is pursued along one direction, it leads to a scientific understanding of the phenomenal world. By this mode one discovers that the nature of physical reality is very different from what it seems to be at first blush. Every observed and experienced physical phenomenon has an inner cause that is veiled from our normal perception.

When pursued along another line, the quest leads to spiritual awakening as to the true nature of ultimate reality. One discovers that beneath and beyond the ephemeral reality of the perceived world, there is a permanent imperishable substratum which alone is real. In other words, ultimate reality is very different from what one is led to believe on the basis of sensory perceptions.

It may be recalled here that in one school of Indian philosophy, there are different kinds of perception. These include the immediate perception of things, understanding what one perceives, perception of the self, and perception of the Divine.

12.1

விலங்கு மனத்தால், விமலா உனக்கு

vilaṅgu manattāl vimalā unakku

With enchained mind, to you, oh unblemished one

Word Meanings

vilaṅgu - enchained/animal-like

manattāl - with the mind

vimalā - blemishless

unakku - to you

Explanatory Reflections

The poet says here that the very nature of the mind is an obstacle that hinders the recognition of its connection with the Divine. In this sense the mind is enchained. One meaning of word *vilaṅgu* is shackles. Thus the poet is suggesting that as long as the mind is fettered by its attachment to the things and pleasures of the world, it is unable to see the Divine. Conversely, as long as we are bereft of the awareness of our spiritual dimension, we are in effect chained. It is as if our mind is in a prison, unable to experience the fullness of freedom that comes from the full understanding and experience of our connections with the cosmic whole. We are reminded here of people confined in Plato'd cave where, seeing mere shadows and taking them to be real, the denizens are unable to even picture the world of light outside of the cave.

These chains that bind us to this world are like golden fetters, for they do glitter and have their charms. But, as Edmund Spenser wrote:

A fool I do him firmly hold,
That loves his fetters, though they were of gold.

Another meaning of the word *vilaṅgu* is animal. This line could also mean that the mind is still in its animal phase as it is unable to recognize its true glory which is its divine attribute. This could be because it has not evolved to a higher level of awareness, or because it has been in this condition for too long. It is interesting to recall in this context something that the Latin writer Tacitus wrote because it combines both these meanings of vilaṅgu: *Etiam fera animalia, si clausa teneas, virtutis, obliviscuntur*: Even wild animals, if you keep them imprisoned, forget their natural courage. Likewise, minds that are kept in chains for long by passions and attachments, forget their intrinsic nature and potential.

What the mystic is saying about the condition for spiritual awakening is equally true in the non-spiritual world. Whether it is good nature or bad, whether it is love for what is noble and elevating, or what is base and ignoble that draws us, depends to a large degree on what we have become accustomed to. That is why good education and development of good taste and habits ought to occur at an early stage of development. If this does not happen in the formative period, it is very difficult to start it all at a later phase of life. The metaphor of a mind that has been enchained or of a creature that has not evolved is a very powerful one here.

12.2

கலந்த அன்பாகிக் கசிந்து உள் உருகும்

kalanda anbāgik kasindu uḷ urugum

mingled with love, the tender heart melts

Word Meanings

kalanda - mingled

anbu - love

āgi - becoming

kasindu - having become tender/soft

uḷ - heart, spirit

urugum - melting

Explanatory Reflections

No matter how much knowledge a person possesses, how keen a mind and how rational his thoughts, as long as one has no feelings for others, no compassion or kindness, and one is unmoved by the sufferings of others, we may say that the person has a heart hard as stone. All too often people spend their lives in self-centered and callous stone-heartedness.

But a change occurs when love enters the heart. Then there is a profound transformation in the attitude and behavior of the individual. In poetic metaphor this is described as the melting of the heart, for it evokes the image of love flowing out of it. For love is not a static entity that stays within, but is the transfer of good thoughts and feelings towards others.

In its grandest manifestation, when love directs all our energies towards the Divine, it is known as *bhakti* in the Hindu tradition. In the *bhakti* mode, we seek truth at the highest level, and swear loyalty to the Supreme. In *An Hymn in Honor of Lov*e, where he also referred to love as a "sweet passion," Edmund Spenser captured this idea succinctly when he wrote:

For Love is lord of truth and loyalty
Lifting himself up out of the lowly dust
On golden plumes up to the purest sky
Above the reach of loathly sinful dust.

But then who implants this love in the human heart and thus transforms it? In this line our poet says that it is the Divine principle that does it. Indeed one might say that the heart that melts by the power of love is a truly blessed one. We are reminded of the verse from a poem which says:

And when my heart melts within me,
and weakness takes control;
God gathers me in His arms,
And soothes my heart and soul.

12.3

நலம் தான் இலாத சிறியரேற்கு நல்கி

nalam tān ilāda chiṟiyēṟku nalgi

Showing grace to petty ones who are without any good

Word Meanings

nalam - good

tān - any

ilāda - being without

chiṟiyēṟku - to a petty one

nalgi - having given/shown grace

Explanatory Reflections

In his poem The Fairy, the poet Shelley wrote:

The virtuous man,
Who, great in his humility as kings
Are little in their grandeur; he who leads
Invincibly a life of resolute good…

Humility is good in ordinary people, but it is very impressive in extraordinary ones. Most simple people are humble for they realize their modest life. Those who have achieved a little tend to vaunt their accomplishments, and become laughable when they do this in excess. When a truly great one displays pride, we may tolerate it because the one with pride may have genuine merit and great success.

However, when such a one is unassuming and humble, our respect for the person is considerably enhanced.

We recognize what a great poetic genius the author of Sivapurāṇam is. We know that he was a saintly person who had reached the highest level of spiritual enlightenment. And when he describes himself as a *nallāntān chiṟiyan*: a petty one with nothing good at all, we are awe-struck indeed.

If this saintly poetic genius calls himself thus, what are we, more ordinary mortals, compared to him? Clearly, this line in this great work reminds us of our own insignificance in the larger scheme of things.

Of course, the poet does not say this to teach us humility. Rather it was the genuine self-appraisal of one who had experienced the Divine. We are humble before a great person, not out of custom or convention, but because the sheer grandeur of the other person imposes that humility on us.

If you run into a truly great individual (scientist, artist, writer, whatever), you are not likely to feel humble if you knew nothing about that individual. But as soon as you get an inkling of how great that personage is, your reaction is likely to be different. Unless we know the greatness of what we are experiencing or confronting, we simply cannot feel this humility. Thus what the poet says here is a reflection of his having recognized the Divine.

12.4

நிலம் தன்மலே் வந்து அருளி நீள்கழல்கள் காட்டி

Nilam tanmēl vandu aruḷ i nīḷ kazalgaḷ kāṭṭi

Coming to earth, you blessed us and showed your majestic feet

Word Meanings

Nilam tanmēl - on land/earth

vandu - having come

aruḷi - giving grace

nīḷ - long/powerful

kazalgaḷ - feet

kāṭṭi - showing

Explanatory Reflections

As noted earlier, to one unfamiliar with the Hindu tradition, the veneration of God's feet might sound strange. In the Hindu framework the feet of God and of any person of high spiritual stature are worshipped. On speaks of *pādapūja*i: worship of the feet.

In the same spirit, when one prostrates to the icon of god, or to an elder, one touches the feet. One interpretation is that we recognize our own lowly status with respect to the person honored. In other words it is a mark of humility.

Cleaning the feet of an honored personage is

also a custom in the culture, with parallels in some other ancient cultures. In Hindu weddings there is a symbolic cleaning of the feet of the bridegroom as he enters the place of wedding. This is done because on that occasion he is regarded as a manifestation of Shiva or Vishṇu.

There is the belief that when the feet touch the bare ground they draw in some of the energy from the earth. In particular, this energy is believed to enter through the toe and the heel.

There are references to foot-washing of saints as mark of adoration, and of kings as mark of respect in the Christian tradition.

When the poet mentions the length of the feet of the Lord, it is of the power and majesty of the Divine that he speaks. There is an ancient belief that the length of a person's feet is an indication of his strength. There is a reference in the *Histories of Herodotus* in which Pythagoras is said to have estimated the strength of Hercules by the length of his feet. Recall the Latin saying *Ex pede Herculem,* translated into English as (you recognize) Hercules by his foot, meaning that his feet were really very large. It is said that in the first Olympic stadium a race was one stade long which was supposed to have been 600 Herculean feet, which was about 633 feet in today's measure. This means that 1 herculean foot = 12.6 inches. Very few people have a foot which is more than 10.5 inches long.

When the poet here says, "coming to earth, you blessed us," he is making an allusion to the appearance of Siva with his contingent in Tirupperundurai. This is the vision that Māṅikkavāsakar had. For this reason the saint-poet continues to be venerated in the temple of Āthmanāthaswami.

12.5

நாயிற் கடையாய்க் கிடந்த அடியேற்கு

nāyiṟ kaḍaiyāi kiḍanda aḍiyēṟku

To the slave who lay being inferior to a dog

Word Meanings

nāyiṟ - to a dog

kaḍaiyāi - being inferior

kiḍanda – was lying

aḍiyēṟku - to the slave

Explanatory Reflections

Here the poet refers to himself as having been inferior to a dog. It is true that for quite a few centuries dogs were regarded as impure and not very respectable. Even today, calling a person a god is a derogatory expression of contempt in many Indian languages.

One might think that the dog was always regarded as a lowly animal in the tradition. However, in Vedic times these creatures had favorable roles in the legends. The great Indra had a canine companion with the name *Saramā*, Two four-eyed dogs are pictured as Yamā's watchdogs. In the Mahabharata, Yudhishtira's dog was first refused admission into Heavan, but then he refued to go there if that was the case. Then the dog (which was Dharma in disguise) was allowed to come also.

Then why does the poet refer to himself as worse than a dog? Perhaps it is to remind us that just as a dog is always loyal and faithful to his master, so must we be to the Divine. And if we are not, if we spend our years with gross indifference to our master, which is the Divine, then of course we become even worse than a dog. Even when we are in such a pathetic state, Divinity comes to save us.

The poet suggests in this line that we humans are sometimes less faithful to God than dogs are to us. Recall the verse by Stephen Collins which says:

Old dog Tray's ever faithful
Grief cannot drive him away;
He's gentle, he's kind; I'll never, never find
A better friend than old dog Tray.

Our devotion to God is seldom as strong and consistent as the dog mentioned here. Perhaps that is what our poet is suggesting when he says that he was for many years lying worse than a dog: that is to say, living a life that was utterly indifferent to and negligent of the very existence of God. But if and when such a person happens to discover God, that is, if and when one intensely experiences the joy and ecstasy that come from a recognition of the Divine, then he/she not only realizes what a glorious experience that is, but also regrets the past years when life was without that joy and ecstasy. It is then that one regrets the many wasteful years of existence.

There is an old saying that the dog is the only animal that has seen his God. Our poet says that a man who hasn't seen his God is worse than a dog.

13.1

தாயிற் சிறந்த தயா ஆன தத்துவனே

tāyir̲ chir̲anda dayā āna tattuvanē

Oh Lord of Nature, more magnificent in compassion than mother!

Word Meanings

tāyir̲ - more than mother

chir̲anda - great, magnificent

dayā āna - as compassion

tattuvanē - oh Lord of Nature (a name for Shiva)

Explanatory Reflections

In the course of our lives we show kindness and compassion to many people. We are also the recipients of kindness and compassion from others. But of all those who show us kindness and compassion none is greater than our mother. That is why one of the first things taught to a Tamil child is that mother and father are the first known Gods: *annaiyum pitāvum munnar̲i deivam.*

In the words of the poetess Sarah Buell Hale,

There is none
In all this cold and hollow world, no fount
Of deep, strong, deathless love,
Save that within a mother's heart.

But is there anyone greater even than mother in this regard? Certainly, Divinity is that one, says the poet in this line.

We may note in passing that the love and compassion that a mother (Mary) shows to God (Jesus) is represented in the famous sculpture of Michelangelo known as *La Pietà*.

Traditionally one lists seven modes by which acts of goodness may be expressed for the body and seven for the spirit. These are called *dayāvirutti*. For the body, these are said to be food, drink, clothing, home, freedom, removal of the constraints of enchainment, proper treatment of the body after death. For the mind, these are: education, solace, mercy, trust, non-envy, not bearing grudge and returning good for evil, praying for the well-being of others.

One of the many names for Lord Shiva is *tattuvan*. It is interesting to inquire into this name. In Tamil the word *tattuvam* also refers to the powers of Nature. The word *tattuvanūl* refers to physics. The school of thought which regards Nature as God is known as *tattuvavādam*.

13.2

மாசற்ற சோதி மலர்ந்த மலர்ச்சுடரே

māchaṯra chōdi malarnda malarchuḍarē

Oh spotless, splendid, blossomed flowery brilliance!

Word Meanings

māchu - spot/stain

aṯra - without

chōdi - light/splendor

malarnda - blossomed

malar - flower

chuḍarē - oh brilliance

Explanatory Reflections

In the next few lines the poet gives some laudatory epithets of the Divine. Everything in the world has some blemish or another, whether human made or in nature. There is nothing in the world that is perfect and flawless. That state of perfection and flawlessness is the attribute only of the Divine. That state is not here in this world of matter and energy, but in the transcendental realm beyond. In a more mundane sense, we speak of the flaws in a person. A wit once wrote:

'Tis one of human nature's laws
To see ourselves without our flaws.

This is a sad, but true commentary on human

nature. However, for the enlightened soul this is not the case. Our poet reminds us here that the only entity that is without any stain or blemish is the Divine.

One might ask, how can light blossom and how can brilliance be flowery? In the ecstatic mood of praising the Divine, poetic license is used in mixed metaphors. When the poet speaks of a blossomed light of flowery brilliance, he expresses most effectively the glorious effulgence of the Divine.

The word *chōdi* in Tamil is actually the *jyoti* of Sanskrit. It thus connotes something more than physical light. *Jyoti* connotes the spiritual aspect of light, the radiance that emanates from a spiritual entity.

In the framework of Hindu esoteric disciplines, when the occult *kuṇḍalinī* energy present in the human body is gradually awakened, an inner illumination (*prakāsha*) leads to the spiritual radiance called *jyoti*. It is said to be the manifestation in the human body of this cosmic effulgence. It is to this that our poet makes reference in this line. It is on this that one meditates while uttering the *gāyatri mantra*.

This invocation reminds us of a strange kind of light that astronomers spotted in the 1990s. It was reported thus (Time Magazine August 13, 1999): “It isn't visible to the naked eye, and when viewed through a large telescope it looks very much like any of the ordinary cosmic bodies in its celestial neighborhood. But this pinpoint of light is anything but ordinary. Spotted more than three years ago, it seemed at first to be a garden-variety star--but it wasn't. It might have turned out to be an unremarkable galaxy or quasar--but it didn't. Frustrated in their attempts to learn its nature, and even its distance from Earth, astronomers have begun to refer to the mystery object as, well, the ‘mystery object.’"

13.3

தேசனே தேனா் ஆரமுதே சிவபுரானே

tēsanē tēnār amudē siva purānē

Oh illustrious one, oh honeyed ambrosian, Oh dweller in Sivapuram

Word Meanings

tēsanē - oh illustrious one!

tēnār - with honey

amudē - oh ambrosia!

siva - Shiva

puranē - oh, of the town!

Explanatory Reflections

In classical Tamil *tēsan* meant one with radiance (Sanskrit *tejas*). Divinity is described as the source of spiritual light. The Divine is not an entity to be seen, but an inner experience. Mystics have said again and again that the experience of the Divine is ineffable, it can only be enjoyed, like sweetness.

The immortalizing potion *amṟitam* is *amudam* in Tamil. In ancient Greek and Roman traditions this milk of Paradise, as Coleridge called it, is the food of the gods which made them immortal. In Hindu sacred history, it was churned out by devas and asuras from the ocean in.

In this line the poet describes the Divine as honeyed ambrosia, meaning that the Divine is both sweet and immortal. What is meant is that those who have experienced the Divine, i.e. have attained the highest spiritual level (*siddhi*) experience ecstasy and have also become immortal. For them, the prayer *mṟityōmā amṟitam gamaya* (From Death lead us to Immortality) has been answered.

We refer to a person in terms of the city or the country from which the person has come: Canadian, Australian, Kolkattan, Keralite, etc. In the Hindu mythic vision, Siva is the Lord of the realm called *Sivapuram* (*Shivaloka*). Hence he is addressed here as *Sivapurān*: one of the city (realm) of Shiva.

The Book of Genesis says, "And God said let there be Light: and there was light." This refers to physical light. The light mentioned by our poet is spiritual light. This too is referred to in the Bible where is says (John 5.35), "He was a burning and shining light." And in Matthew (5. 14), "You are the light of the world." The motto of the Catholic University of America is *Deus lux mea*: God is my light. Thus, in all spiritual traditions the Divine has been experienced as Light. The Qur'an (24.35) describes God as "the light of the heavens and the earth.".

MANIKKAVASAKAR'S SIVAPURANAM

13.4

பாசமாம் பற்று அறுத்துப் பாரிக்கும் ஆரியனே

pāsamām paṯṟu aṟuttup pārikkum āriyanē

Oh Master, who severs the chain of bondage and appears

Word Meanings

pāsamām - the (triple) bondage

paṯṟu - attachment

aṟuttu - having cut

pārikkum - appearing

āriyanē - oh Master

Explanatory Reflections

In the framework of Saiva Siddhāntam, bondage to the world arises from three sources. These are *āṇavam* pride or ego-sense, *karumam*: consequential action, and *māyai*: illusion. Our sense of pride and ego makes us long for more, our actions invariably bear fruit and cause rebirth, and the illusion that everything is for ever makes us imagine we will always have all these enjoyments and things. They cause attachment to this world. So they are like ropes that bind us.

We will never get out of the cycle unless this rope is cut. Who can do it for us except the Divine principle? It is only when Divinity appears to us, that is to say, it is only when one attains God-realization that this *pāsam,* this rope will be cut off and we will become truly free.

Recall that in the Saiva Siddhāntam framework there is the image of the Lord as the master of all creatures, as of the cattle which the Divine will protect. The word *pasu* has several meanings: one of them is *cow.* Another is a *sentient being.* That is why Lord Siva is called *pasupati* the lord of all sentient beings. Likewise, the difficult-to-sever involvement of the soul with various attachments of the body is known as *pasupāsam.*

Note the word *āriyan* here, derived from the Sanskrit *āryā.* In classical Tamil, it simply meant a scholar or teacher. Sometimes it also meant a medical doctor. Much of the Indian subcontinent was known as *āriyam* (*āryavarta*). Also, the Sanskrit language was called *āriyamozi* which could mean the language of the learned, although some would interpret the word as the language of the *āriyā* people. It is in contexts like this that it is difficult to accept the notion that Tamil and Sanskrit were one and the same language. In our own times, in certain circles it would be politically incorrect to say otherwise. In any case, it is interesting that here the Tamil poet refers to Shiva as *āriyan.*

13.5

நசே அருள்புரிந்து நஞெ்சில் வஞ்சம் கடெ

nēsa aruḷ purindu en neñjil vañcham keḍa

From your friendly grace my illusions are dispelled

Word Meanings

nēsa - affectionate, friendly

aruḷ - grace

purindu - having bestowed

en - my

neñjil - in the heart/mind

vañcham - lie, deceit

keḍa - may perish

Explanatory Reflections

An interesting feature of Saiva Siddhāntam (as of Hindu theology) is that on the one hand Divinity is pictured in cosmic and abstract terms, and on the other hand, Divinity is a very personal, even geographically localized, God who interacts with individuals as a caring friend. The seeker approaches the Divine Principle with great respect and affection as a student or lover would. This is the *bhakti* mode. In this line, the poet does not refer to himself as a friend, but rather describes God as friendly. The notion of God as a friend of the poor (*dīnabandhu*) is there is the classical *bhakti* framework.

To all appearances, divine grace (*aruḷ*) is not given to everyone, just as one does not give gifts to everyone. That is why the poet describes the *aruḷ* he has received with the adjective *nēsa* - affectionate or loving.

Divine grace is like light that that shines in a pitch-dark room where one has been groping for a long time, misinterpreting what one touches and feels. When the light is lit one realizes how wrong one was in the apprehensions. With the awakening that comes from divine grace one begins to see the world in an entirely different framework. The poet is suggesting that when divine grace comes upon a person, all the mental and moral impurities, all the lies and deceits perpetrated on the mind through the veil of *māyā* will melt away even as the morning sun dispels the dark of the night.

We are reminded here of what the Dalai Lama said: "If we can realize and meditate on ultimate truth, it will cleanse our impurities of mind." This idea is also implicit in the Upanishadic prayer: *tamasōmā jyōtir gamaya*: From Darkness lead us to Light. Our poet says that the same thing will happen if and when we receive Divine grace. Again and again we see that we are reading the utterings of a mystical poet who pours out from his heart.

We may recall in this context the lines of the poet R. W. Gilder (*The New Day*):

Against the darkness outer,
God's light, His likeness takes,
And he from the mighty doubter
The great believer makes.

14.1

பேராது நின்ற பெருங்கருணைப் பேராறே

pērādu ninḍṟa paruṅkaruṇaip pōrāṟē

Oh all-embracing river of mercy who envelops

Word Meanings

pēr - excellent

ādu - river

ninḍṟa - which stood

perum - great

karuṇai - mercy

pōrāṟē - oh enveloping river

Explanatory Reflections

Rivers have been great blessings for agriculture, and make lands fertile. They have also been blessings for culture and civilization. We have only to think of the Nile and the Po, of Kāveri and Ganga to realize this. Through their silent flow and graceful meandering rivers enhance the beauty of the landscape.

In Hindu culture the river has been compared to the paths chosen by people to pray and worship. We are reminded that just as waters falling from the skies go to the ocean (as rivers) (*ākāshāt patitantōyam yathā gacchadi sāgaram*) prostrations to all gods (*sarva deva namaskārah*) go back to the same Divinity (*kēshavam pratigacchadi*). The word river brings to mind a steady stream of water that never fails.

The age-long flow of rivers, bringing water to the people all along its way, cool the land, quench the thirst, and nourish the plants that grow the needed food. Rivers are therefore like the constant outpouring of love and kindness. So the poet describes the Divine in this line as a superb river through which God's mercy is for ever flowing. As the Divine is the source of all the blessings we receive, it is spoken of here as a grand river surging with the clear water of kindness and compassion.

Countless poets and thinkers have evoked and extolled water. Recall St. Exupēry's reflection (*Wind, Sand and Stars*): "Water, thou hast no taste, no color, no odor; canst not be defined, art relished while ever mysterious. Not necessary to life, but rather life itself, thou fillest us with a gratification that exceeds the delight of the senses." Or again. G. W. Curtin wrote, "A river is the coziest of friends. You must love it and live with it before you can know it." What an apt description in this context!

We may recall that Maṇikkavāsakar lived in the Tamil country which was blessed with many rivers. In his Tiruvāsakam too he compares Divinity to a river.

14.2

ஆரா அமுதே அளவிலாப் பெம்மானே

ārā amudē aḷavilāp pemmānē

Never-satiating immeasurable great God!

Word Meanings

ārā - never satiating

amudē - oh nectar

aḷavilā - measureless

pemmānē - oh God!

Explanatory Reflections

It is poetic and customary to use sweetness and nectar as similes and metaphors for what we enjoy immensely. But the things we enjoy in the world have one limitation. Sooner or later we tire of them. Whether it is the most delicious food or games we play or the movies we see, or even whether it is the music we listen to, the books we are fond of, or whatever, experiencing these again and again can become tiring sooner or later, and we will yearn for something else.

This is especially true of sweet and sugary things. There is a Tamil word for this: *tevittugiṟēn*: I feel nauseated because of the excess, usually of something saccharine. The word for nauseating is sometimes changed into *tegiṭṭugiṟadu* in colloquial Tamil.

Recall Shakespeare's line in Henry IV:

They surfeited with honey and began
To loath the taste of sweetness whereof a little
More than a little is by much too much.

A Tamil maxim pithily says, *aḷavukku miñjināl amirudamum visham*: In excess, even ambrosia is poison. Excess is when something goes beyond full capacity.

The poet says here that the nectar that is Divinity is an exception to this rule: it can never be over-filling, tiring, or nauseating. Unlike with candy and caramel, we can never feel we have had more than we can take of it. The Divine is measureless: that is to say, infinite in scope. The Latin poet Horace wrote, *Est modus in rebus:* There is a measure in all things. However, exclaims our poet, this does not apply to God. There can be a measure of humans and worldly things, but there is no measure of God, much less of the nectar that is divine experience, of blessed ecstasy.

Pemmān is a contraction of *perumān*: Great God. Literally, it simply refers to a great personage, an anthropic image of *Purushottama* of the Sanskrit tradition.

14.3

ஓராதார் உள்ளத்து ஒளிக்கும் ஒளியானே

ōrādār uḷḷ attuḷ oḷikkum oḷiyānē

Oh Luminous One that shines in the hearts of even those
who know not!

Word Meanings

ōrādār - who don't know, don't consider

uḷḷattuḷ - in the hearts

oḷikkum - shining

oḷiyānē - oh luminous one!

Explanatory Reflections

Not everyone is God-conscious. Few take the time to even consider the presence or the role of God in their lives. They do their routine chores, and live a mechanical existence with neither time nor interest for matters religious, metaphysical, or spiritual. In this line the poet says that Divinity is present even in the hearts of such people. It is like a light that is shining within each and every one of us, for at the deepest core, that is what we all are: a spark of the Divine. This is also the essence of the teachings of the Upanishads.

Consider the forces of nature. Not many people

think of them consciously. For example, how many reflect seriously on gravitation? Yet everyone is subject to it. How many know the nature of heat or light? Yet we all see things and we all feel hotness. Thoughtful awareness of universal principles is not a necessary condition for our being under their sway.

Or again, there are myriad activities going on in our bodies that keep us alive. But even if we don't care to investigate how the heart beats, how the neurons fire, how enzymes are generated and hormones secreted, how cells divide and subdivide, we continue to live.

We are told that the same is true of the Divinity in us. It is that which sustains our existence and integrity as human beings. Without it there would be neither life not thought nor consciousness. It is the like the electric power that keeps the light burning.

We are reminded in this line that at the very least, in the basic aspect of sustenance we all receive that grace from God, for were it not for the marvelous balance of the biological processes that keep the body functioning we cannot live even for a fleeting moment. All that is also possible because of the external balance in our planetary environment.

Being unaware of these does not negate their presence. Even those who know nothing of oxygen breathe and live. Even those who nothing of plant botany and grain chemistry eat and ingest their food. That is the message in this line. We must not only not forget this, but also be grateful for this. That is the deeper significance of prayer, the deeper goal of meditation. Once we realize this and see a ray of that transcendental effulgence in our fellow human beings, not only does it become impossible to hate or treat anyone harshly, we develop love and respect for one and all.

14.4

நீராய் உருக்கி என் ஆருயிராய் நின்றானே

nīrāi urukki en āruyirāi nindṟānē

Oh, He stood, as the fullness of my soul was fluidly molten

Word Meanings

nīrāi - as liquid
urukki - melting
en - my
āruyirāi - as fullness of soul
nindṟānē - oh, he stood

Explanatory Reflections

Thomas À Kempis spoke of the *duritia cordis humani*: hardness of the human heart. Indeed, we often refer to people without compassion as hard-hearted. Such people are not easily moved by the finer feelings of love and kindness. We also describe as soft-hearted those who are easily moved by the suffering and pain of others.

When a hard-hearted person changes into one of a gentler kind, it is as if a hard solid has slowly softened. In the poetic imagery, it is as if something very metallic and sturdy is gradually melting away. A folk songs from *Tiruttōnōkkam* says: *kal pōlum neñcam kasindurugi*: Like a stone the heart was moistening and melting.

Such a profound transformation can occur only by the grace of the Divine. No matter how we explain human behavior, through genes, brain chemistry, neurotransmitters, or whatever, ultimately the question of how these have come to act in so many positive ways cannot be answered in the framework of science alone. Nor is it explained by the poetic and religious vision, one might say. But religious visions add meaning and beauty to what is experienced.

The poet goes on to say that the Divine melted his soul and made it a more complete one. A life that is unmoved and uncaring is an incomplete unfulfilled one. The meaning is that only when we are touched by nobler sentiments and we care for others that we become fuller human beings. The poet is suggesting here that when a person becomes more than for his or her own selfish survival, we may be sure that the person has been truly blessed with the grace of Divinity. It is then that our souls beome truly full, that is to say we are really fulfilled.

We are reminded of Mother Teresa's words: "Faith is more important to me than life itself because without it there would be no fullness of life."

Teresa of Avila said: "God speaks to souls

through words uttered by pious people, by sermons or good books, and in many other such ways." Māṅikkavāsakar was one of those voices through which God speaks.

14.5

இன்பமும் துன்பமும் இல்லானே உள்ளானே

inbamum tunbamum illānē uḷḷānē

One who is with and without joys and sorrows

Word Meanings

inbamum - both joy

tunbamum - and suffering

illānē - one who is without

uḷḷānē - one who is with

Explanatory Reflections

There is more to existence than breathing and surviving. Life is interesting and worthwhile because of the little pleasures and joys that it offers. However, there is no life without pain and suffering either. William Cowper expressed the thoughts of many reflecting people (*The Poplar Field*):

To muse on the perishing pleasures of man:
Though his life be a dream, his enjoyments, I see,
Have a being less durable than he.

Or again, recall the lines of Francis Thompson (*Daisy*):

Nothing begins, and nothing ends,
That is not paid with moan;
For we are born in others' pain,
And perish in our own.

In Tamil the positive experiences of life are known as *inbam*. The negative experiences are called *tunbam*. And we are all are subjected to both.

The poet says that Divinity is beyond all the constraints of pleasure and pain. This seems an appropriate description of the Almighty, God is transcendental. However, the poet also says that the Divine has both joys and sorrows. Being pure bliss, God may well be described as with joy. But what about pain? Perhaps it is in what God feels for humanity, His compassion for all creatures. When all the suffering and pain the world is taken into account, the pity and compassion of no single individual will suffice to encompass it all. In this context, the symbolism of Christ is powerful, for it evokes the vision of God taking upon Himself all the pain and suffering of humankind. The same may be said of the Budha who felt deeply for the sufferings of others, and of Mahavira who felt likewise for all creatures.

Those who have truly experienced God know ecstasy, but they also feel the suffering and anguish of their fellow creatures. If some of us mortals feel the pain of fellow creatures, it is not unreasonable to say that God too has his pains. As C. S. Lewis said (*The Probmem of Pain*), "God whispers to us in our pleasures, speaks in our conscience, but shouts in our pains."

15.1

அன்பருக்கு அன்பனே யாவையுமாய் இல்லையுமாய்

anbarukku anbanē yāvaiyumāi illaiyumāmāi

Friend of friends, all and nothing too

Word Meanings

anbarukku - to friends

anbanē - oh friend

yāvaiyum - also whatever

āi - becoming

illaiyum - nothing

āi – becoming

Explanatory Reflections

The word *anbu* literally means *love.* Whence *anban* connotes one who loves. But this word has two other meanings: *husband,* and friend. In the *bhakti* mode where the aspirant is in total love with God, one regards oneself as a lover and as a friend of God. When one befriends God, God becomes one's friend: so declares the poet in this line.

But then, this is only natural. If you are friendly to someone that person normally reciprocates your friendship. But with God, says the poet in this line, it is much more. God becomes not only a friend, but practically everything one can imagine. When he says God becomes everything the poet is suggesting that when one enters into a mystic merger with God, one sees the Divine spirit everywhere and in everything in the world. It is not a case of God's omnipresence, but God *becoming* everything. From this perspective, the created world is not a product of the Divine, but its transformation.

There is something more: The Divine will not stay for ever in these manifest forms. In other words, Divinity will also become the no-ness (*allai*) of it all. That is to say, the enlightened soul will not only see the Divine in everything, but also recognize that these are the passing phases of the Divine, and are not to be taken as its ultimate manifestations.

Thus the mystically awakened person realizes two things about perceived reality: Everything that is happening here is an embodiment of the Divine. And yet, it is an ephemeral embodiment, for its aspect in the configuration will be constantly changing, until it is completely dissolved.

This line also reminds us of the traditional prayer, *tvamēva bandhu cha sakhā tvamēva*: You (God) indeed are my kin and my friend.

In the Bible we read (John 15:15) that Jesus once said:

I no longer call you servants, because a servant does not know his master's business. Instead, I have called you friends, for everything that I learned from my Father I have made known to you.

Regarding God as friend is another way of saying that one trusts completely in God. Saying that we are God's friend means that we should be worthy of his trust.

15.2

சோதியனே துன்னிருளே தோன்றாப் பெருமையனே

chōdiyanē tunniruḷē tōnḍṟāp perumaiyanē

Oh radiant one, oh great one near whom no darkness comes!

Word Meanings

chōdiyanē - oh radiant one!

tun - nearby

iruḷē - darkness

tōnḍṟā - not appearing

perumaiyanē - oh eminent one!

Explanatory Reflections

As we have seen before, the radiant light coming from a mystical source is *chōdi* (Sanskrit *jyoti*). One who radiates it is a *chōdiyan*. Here the poet addresses the Divine with this word because that is where spiritual effulgence comes from. Again and again, those who have had a vision of the Divine have described it as blinding effulgence.

Or again, recall the line in the Bhagavad Gita where it describes the Divine as *ādityavarṅam tamasah parastāt* (VIII.9): the color of the sun (radiant as the sun) and beyond darkness.

Consider any object: a building or a tree, a mountain or even the moon. Every one of them can cast a shadow. Thus it is possible to associate darkness with all these bodies when they stand in the path of light. The obstruction of light is what causes darkness. But we cannot even imagine the shadow of the sun. The sun simply cannot have a shadow of its own. Darkness is nowhere near the radiant sun, for it is the sun that dispels all darkness around it. So it is with the Divine. Its radiance removes all darkness, it melts the veil of ignorance, it reveals the true nature of Reality. In other words, God is light sublime and pure.

Recall the thought of Ralph Waldo Emerson (*the Oversoul*): "From within or from behind, a light shines through us upon things, and makes us aware that we are nothing, but the light is all." Therein lies the recognition of the Divine.

The vision of God as pure radiance is not unique to the Hindu tradition. We read about God in the Old Testament as "Who coverest thyself with light as with a garment..." In the Bible there are several references to God as light, the light of the world, heaven being full of light, etc. Milton wrote in his *Paradise Lost*:

God is light
And never but in unapproached light
Dwelt from eternity.

15.3

ஆதியனே அந்தம் நடுவாகி அல்லானே

ādiyanē antam naḍuvāgi allānē

Oh Origin of all, one without middle and end

Word Meanings

ādiyanē - oh Origin

antam - end

naḍuvāgi - becoming middle

allānē - oh, One without (that)

Explanatory Reflections

Everything in the world has a, origin (a beginning) and an end. But there is an exception to this. Divinity has neither a beginning, nor an end. That is why the two most telling epithets for God are *anādi*: beginning-less, and *anantam*: end-less. For a straight line, however long, there is a mid-point. But this is true only of any finite line. If the line is infinite, then it has neither an end nor a beginning, and no middle either. So it is with the Divine. It is a sophisticated mathematical insight that the infinite is without a middle.

Another visualizable analogy would be the circle. The circumference of a circle has no beginning point, no middle point and no end point. In addition, the circle is also the perfect geometrical figure. Thus Divine may be pictured as cosmic perfection, with neither beginning, middle, end, nor blemish.

With the number system there is something interesting: If we take all integers between 1 and say, 1000, there is a beginning (1), an end (1000), and also a middle (500). But if we consider the totality of all integers, positive and negative, from minus infinity to plus infinity, there is no beginning or end, and the middle would be zero: the most powerful of them all.

Though Divinity has no beginning or end, it is itself the beginning of everything. Nothing ever emerged in the world except from God. This notion has been expressed by other poets as well. Thus, Alexander Pope wrote in his *Universal Prayer*: "Thou Great First Cause, least understood." We may recall the very first Kuṟaḷ :

akara mudal ezuttellām ādi bagavan mudaṯṟ e ulagu

First in alphabets is the sound of A,
First in the World, Source-God does stay.

Or again, we may recall what it says in *Revelations*: I am alpha and omega, the beginning and the ending, saith the Lord.

The Latin poet Marcus Fabius Quintilian wrote (Oratoria: V, 10): "Deficit omne quod nascitur:

Everything ends that has a beginning." One may say likewise, That with has no beginning has no end." In the terminology of current cosmology the Divine is beyond the initial singlularity which wrupted into the Bog Bang.

15.4

ஈர்த்து என்னை ஆட்கொண்ட எந்தை பெருமானே

īrttu ennai ātkoṇḍa endai perumānē

Oh great Lord who drew and accepted me!

Word Meanings

īrttu - drawing towards

ennai - me

ātkoṇḍa - who accepted as a devotee

endai - my father

perumānē - oh great Lord!

Explanatory Reflections

On more than one occasion we have seen that the poet is referring to his spiritual transformation as an unexpected blessing rather than as something he had been striving for.

Thus, in this line the poet says that the Divine had drawn him towards it, rather than that he was attracted to it. He also says that having been drawn, he had been accepted as a deep-devotee of God, implying that not all who enter a place of worship are so transformed. Clearly, the state of being an ardent worshiper of God at the level of the sage-poet is a privilege that is not given to everyone. Such piety is surely an expression of God's grace. The poet says, in effect: Here, but for the grace of

God, I would not be.

All too often, we regard the positive things we receive in life as fruits of our own actions, talents, and unusual abilities. Such a view is tainted by unwarranted pride. For, if we pause to think, we will realize that those talents, abilities, and inclinations arose from factors over which we had no control: genes, parentage, family environment, and the like. Every positive experience in life may be regarded as a blessing. Even viewing these as kārmic consequences of commendable actions in past lives, if we were to trace sufficiently back in rebirths, they must have had indeterminate origins. In a game of cards, the player does exercise his or her talents and intelligence. But the hand that is dealt, the cards one gets in a distribution after the shuffle, is beyond anyone's control. It is, in a sense, a blessing.

Here, as elsewhere, the poet addresses God as *endai*: My Father, for, like a father, God draws the aspirant towards him with guiding love. The use of this phrase is like as the Christian Lord's Prayer where it says: *Pater noster*: Our Father, or avinu (אבינו) in Hebrew. This reveals the commonalty among spiritual aspirants in all traditions. If, in a previous line he said *sahā tvamēva* (you are indeed a friend), here he says *tvamēva pitā* (you are indeed a father).

Note that in the case of our poet, this plea to God has already been answered.

15.5

கூர்த்த மெய் ஞானத்தால் கொண்டு உணர்வார் தம்கருத்தில்

kūrtta mei ñānattāl koṇḍuṇarvār tam karuttil

Through keen wisdom will they know its significance.

Word Meanings

kūrtta - keen, sharp

mei - truth

ñanattal - with wisdom

koṇḍuṇarvār - will realize/become aware of, with

tam - its

karuttil – in the meaning, significance

Explanatory Reflections

In the framework of Saiva Siddhāntam there are four *neṟi* or paths available to the spiritual aspirant. These are:

(a) *sariyai* which is the first step that the initiate takes under the guidance of a guru, qualifying him for simple worship.

(b) *kiriyai* which refers to action, qualifying him to do daily *pūjai* (worship service) for Siva as per the rituals.

(c) *yōgam* which refers to yogic meditation at an abstract level.

(d) *ñānam* which is the state attained by Shaiva

ascetics who have l all their mundane desires, conquered their passions, and are ready to become one with the Siva principle. This highest level of wisdom is also called *meiññānam* or *sanmārkkam* which is the path of the spiritually illumined jñāni.

This wisdom is razor-sharp, hence the phrase *kūrtta meiññānam.* One who has attained it will regard all other knowledge as ordinary, if not trivial, just as to the erudite scholar cannot take too seriously a child's book of stories.

The *meiñjñānis* have deep awareness of what it is all about. From their loftier perspective all the passing show of the world is but a simple game, and does not deserve too serious an attention. One begins to see what is not observable to the superficial and unrealized person. There is a famous quote from Jonathan Swift: "Vision is the art of seeing the invisible."

A small room looks confined to one who has stood on the summit of a tall mountain and surveyed the panorama all around. Spiritual realization implies a deeper understanding and recognition of the ultimate nature of reality which arises from the lofty perspective.

16.1

நோக்கரிய நோக்கே நுணுக்கரிய நுண் உணர்வே

nōkkariya nōkkē nuṇukkariya nuṇ uṇarvē

One Who is difficult to focus on, and subtle to grasp

Word Meanings

nōkku - gaze

ariya - difficult

nōkkē - oh focus of concentration

nuṇukku - minute

ariya - difficult

nuṇ - subtle

uṇarvē - understanding

Explanatory Reflections

Experience shows that when we try to direct our minds to something and hold it there for some time, it becomes extremely difficult to maintain the concentration. This is true of any matter, and yet this concentration is essential if we are to achieve anything of significance. The difficulty in concentrating becomes all the more so when the focus of our thoughts is the Divine principle. The mind wavers and is distracted by a million things. That is why yoga has been defined as the process by which one restrains the incessant changes that characterize the mind.

In this line our poet refers to this fact by saying that it is extremely difficult to fix our (mental) gaze on the Divine principle. That is why this mode of spiritual fulfillment is regarded as the highest and hardest to achieve. Reflective thinkers have often considered the nature of God. They have come up with mounds of descriptions of Divinity. These are great, but they do not really unravel the unfathomable mystery. John Ruskin wrote (*Modern Painters*), "The infinity of God is not mysterious, it is only unfathomable; not concealed, but incomprehensible. It is a clear infinity, the darkness of the pure unsearchable sea."

Our poet says likewise that transcendental truths are too subtle to be grasped by the powers of the intellect. Analysis is good as far as it goes, and can be tremendously valuable in worldly contexts. But they often fail miserably for understanding the Divine. It says in the New Testament (Mark 10:25) that, "It is easier for a camel to go through the eye of a needle than for a rich man to enter into the kingdom of God." Using this simile we might say that it is easier for a rope to pass through the eye of a needle than for the logical analytical mode to grasp the nature of the Divine. We are also reminded of the line in the Guru Granth Sahib where it says (127) :

The unseen and inscrutable Lord is permeating and pervading

everywhere. He cannot be obtained by any effort.

16.2

போக்கும் வரவும் புணர்வும் இலாப் புண்ணியனே

pōkkum varavum puṇarvum illāppuṇṇiyanē

Oh Holy One without entry or exit or links

Word Meanings

pōkkum - going

varavum - and coming

puṇarvum - and connections/links

illā - without

puṇṇiyanē - Oh Holy One

Explanatory Reflections

Consider anything with respect to a place and time. It could be a person and a house, or a planet at a position in the sky. It is possible to say that the entity in question comes into the place or leaves the place at this time or that. Thus a person may leave the house in the morning and return in the evening. A planet may come near the sun at one time of the year and leave that region at another time. Thus everything comes and goes at various places at various times. Tom Stoppard quipped that every exit is an entry into somewhere. This suggests that there is instability and impermanence in exits and entries.

But Divinity is present everywhere at all times.

So the Divine may be described, as the poet does in this line, as one that has no going and coming: This is another feature of infinity.

Every entity in the universe has some link or connection with some other entity or entities. But the Divine encompasses everything. It is in everything (*panentheistic*). Therefore, there is no question of its having particular connection with anything in particular. That is what the poet means when he says that Divinity is without any specific link (*puṇarvam*).

The word *puṇṇiyam* refers to any meritorious act. In the Tamil canonical tradition, one generally lists seven such acts. These are, *nigaṅgkiruti*: being without vanity; *dānam*: giving; *virudam*: periodic abstinence; *sinēkam*: kind behavior; *nayapōsanam*: hospitality; *kamai*: patience; *uṟsāgam*: enthusiasm to do good things. Here, however, the Divine is called the personifation of *puṇṇiyam*. One with all these qualities and more which never fail to become holy.

In the Christian tradition also one speaks of seven virtues: chastity, temperance, charity, diligence, patience, kindness, and humility. These are usually contrasted with the seven deadly sins of lust, gluttony, greed, sloth, wrath, envy, and pride.

16.3

காக்கும் என் காவலனே காண்பரிய பேர் ஒளியே

kākkum en kāvalanē kāṇpariya pēr oḷiyē
Oh my guarding warden, effulgence too bright to behold!

Word Meanings

kākkum - guarding
en - my
kāvalanē - protector
kāṇbu - sight
ariya - difficult
pēr - great
oḷiyē - effulgence

Explanatory Reflections

Among the many functions that traditional religions assign to the Divine is the protection of human beings. In this sense one may look upon God as a guardian of human interests. What does this mean? The first simple meaning is that God takes care of us when we are in difficulty. The poet Byron wrote (*Don Juan: cxcvi*) that no rapture is real as that of one who is watching over "what they love when sleeping." In a peculiar way, when we fall asleep each night, there is really no guarantee that we will wake up the next day, for who knows what circumstance can arise within the body or in our vicinity that might bring life to an end. We go to sleep each night with the implicit certainty that all will be well for us while we are not conscious of our surroundings. This assurance may well be taken as complete faith that we will be protected during our sleep. We are reminded of François Rabelais who said: "I place no hope in my strength, nor in my works: but all my confidence is in God my protector, who never abandons those who have put all their hope and thought in him."

From a larger perspective, the healthy functioning of a body for a few decades depends on a million factors - the biochemistry of processes within the body on the one hand, and the appropriate physical conditions - air pressure, sufficient oxygen in the atmosphere, sufficient ozone in the upper layers of the atmosphere, reasonable periodic rainfall, etc. etc. - in our surroundings. The unseen and unknown factors that individually and collectively sustain all life on earth may well be regarded as what Divine action is all about.

On the one hand, the presence of God in all this may seem as obvious as a flash of light to some. On the other hand, this is not easy for one and all to see. So the poet describes Divinity as the great light that it is difficult to see: *kāṇbariya pēr oḷi*.

16.4

ஆற்றின்ப வெள்ளமே அத்தா மிக்காய் நின்ற

āṯrinba veḷḷamē attā mikkāi ninḍṟa

Oh flooding river of ecstasy, Oh Father Who stands in splendor

Word Meanings

āṯṟu - river

inba – of ecstasy

veḷḷamē - oh flood!

attā - of father!

mikkāi - as great, splendid

ninḍṟa - who stood

Explanatory Reflections

The river is a symbol here of something that is peacefully and happily flowing. That is one reason for using the river-simile for spiritual joy. Another reason is that its waters cleanse the body, as does the spiritual experience.

Then again, spiritual joy is not like any other. It is more than the smoothly flowing current in a river. Spiritual ecstasy is an overwhelming, overpowering gush of the highest kind of joy one can imagine or experience. Therefore, a huge surge of the dynamic river, causing a deluge, brings out the image more clearly. Hence the poet speaks of an ecstatic flood in the river. Also, such a surge of water will cleanse the body thoroughly, leaving no dirt behind, as anyone who has stood on the waves at the beach will know. The image of a flood of divine joy was expressed by the poet Shelly in his *To a Skylark* thus:

Teach us, Sprite or Bird
What sweet thoughts are thine;
I have never heard
Praise of love or wine
That panted forth a flood of rapture so divine.

If the quantitative aspect of the Divine is expressed through the idea of a flood, its qualitative feature is conveyed through the word *mikku* greatness, splendor. Once again, the poet addresses this Divinity of overwhelming splendor as Father, suggesting that ultimately we are all sparks of that universal Divinity. One message of Saiva Siddhāntam is that those who realize this are worthy of our reverence.

We are reminded here of the lines of Jalal ad-Din Rumi (*Desire*) which may be interpreted as the words of the Divine:

I am your lover, come to my side, I will open the gate to your love.
Come settle with me, let us be neighbors to the stars.

You have been hiding so long, endlessly drifting in the sea of my love.
Even so, you have always been connected to me.
Concealed, revealed, in the unknown, in the un-manifest.
I am life itself. You have been a prisoner of a little pond,
I am the ocean and its turbulent flood. Come merge with me,
Leave this world of ignorance.
Be with me, I will open the gate to your love.

16.5

தோற்றச் சுடர் ஒளியாய்ச் சொல்லாத நுண் உணர்வாய்

tōṯṟach chuḍar oḷiyāi chollāda nuṇ uṇarvāi
Who appears as brilliant light, You grasp the most subtle unuttered things.

Word Meanings

tōṯṟa – appearing
chuḍar - brilliant
oḷiyāi - as light, as splendor
chollāda - unspoken, unutterable
nuṇ - subtle
uṇarvāi - you become aware of

Explanatory Reflections

When the poet refers again to the brilliance of the Divine he means the spiritual knowledge that is embodied in Divinity. But the Divine knows and understands everything: Omniscience. The idea is that there is a spiritual splendor that defies easy description, but whose effulgence may be regarded as the subtlest of all that is subtle. And those who know it will not, indeed cannot, speak about it. When Laozi said, "Those who know, speak not; and those who speak, know not," he was not referring to our knowledge of physics or history, but of spiritual truths and truths about God.

On the physical plane, for example, light is brilliant and emanates from the brightest and the most massive objects in the universe. And yet, light itself is the subtlest of all that is subtle. As physicists would say, photons do not carry any mass. But they carry vast amounts of information. It is through light that we come to know about the forms and shapes of things. Interacting with the human sensory system, they add to our aesthetic dimensions as colors. The nature of light itself is extremely complex, and is by no means obvious. We humans try to fathom the essence of light through our instruments and analyses. We also wonder about the origin of things and the future of our universe. Scientists talk about these matters, philosophers argue about them, our religions give us different accounts of origins and ends. But ultimately, can we ever be sure of what we are talking about on these questions? Only the Divine, only spiritual awareness can know the real, the what and why and how of existence. This realization is the highest humility. In other words, what the poet is saying here is that the Divine alone understands the essence of what this is all about, that Ultimate Truth is unimaginably subtle. The Greek philosopher Xenophanes said (*Fragments*), " Pure truth no man has seen, nor ever shall know." Our poet says this in more positive terms: That the Divine alone knows it, indeed that the ultimate truth cannot even be articulated.

It is simply impossible to know through reason and logic the Divine in the way we know atoms and molecules, the sun and the moon. For, in the words of Blaise Pascal (Pensées), "Human beings must be known to be loved; but Divine beings must be loved to be known - *Dieu doit être aimé pour être connu.*"

17.1

மாற்றமாம் வையகத்தின் வெவ்வேறே வந்து அறிவாம்

māṯṟamām vaiyagattin vevvēṟē vandu aṟivām
As various changes in the world, and as knowledge too

Word Meanings

māṯṟamām - changes, again and again
vaiyagattin - on earth, in the world
vevvēṟē - various
vandu - coming
aṟivām - knowledge also

Explanatory Reflections

In this line (which is to be completed in the next) the poet is first referring to the doctrine of re-birth. People do many things, and to reap the fruits of their actions they are born again and again. The variety of reasons for which people are born again is unimaginably large.

Thus, not only is the phenomenon of the cycle of birth and death enormously complex and mysterious, considerably more inscrutable are the particular causes for the birth and death of billions of people. When we reflect on the number (present and past) of human beings who have been coming and going this way, the matter becomes yet another inscrutable mystery in the grand scheme of things. An incredibly powerful supercomputer is needed to store all the relevant data pertaining to this..

The poet has already referred to the omnipresence of God, and to His omnipotence as well. Now he is about to mention God's omniscience as well. It is difficult to even imagine what omniscience signifies. Here we have an instance of what that could be. It is no secret that by definition, God has all the knowledge in the world. But before we think of this infinity, we should consider the infinity of topics on which we could gather information. One of these is the knowledge that each of us possesses. But our own knowledge even about ourselves is extremely limited. We may remember some of our earlier years, certainly not our infancy, and much less the hidden reasons which are responsible for the current phase of our corporeal presence here on earth. Now if we multiply this amount of information by the number of humans who have lived, the variety and range and number of things and events become unimaginably large. But all such knowledge, declares our poet here, is within the scope of Divinity's understanding.

The thought of Divinity's infinity reminds us of

the words of Swami Sivananda (often wrongly attributed to Voltaire):

Meditation is the dissolution of thoughts in eternal awareness or pure consciousness without objectification, knowing without thinking, merging finitude in infinity."

17.2

தேற்றனே தேற்றத் தெளிவே என்
சிந்தனை உள்

tēṯṟanē tēṯṟat teḷivē en chindaiyuḷ

Oh Truthful One (Who brings) clarity to mind!

Word Meanings

tēṯṟanē - oh, certain one! oh comforting one!

tēṯṟam - truthfulness

teḷivē - clarity

en - my

chindaiyuḷ - in mind

Explanatory Reflections

The first word of this line goes with the last one of the previous line. Thus it is *aṟivām tētranē* which could mean, "oh the Knowledge-certain One!" That is to say the Divine alone has all correct and definitive knowledge.

The phrase *tētram koḍuppadu* also means to bring comfort. In this sense, the poet may be referring to the Lord whose invocation brings comfort and calmness to the human heart.

The poet invokes God as the clarity of clarity. The absolutely spotless nature of the Divine is what is lauded here. *Sivajñānam* is like the crème de la crème of all wisdom.

There is, in many of the lines of the

Sivapurāṇam, a beautiful blending of what the Divine is and what a person who is awakened to that Divinity is. Certainty of knowledge and clarity of mind are no doubt attributes of the Shiva principle. But a little of these are also reflected in the minds of those who have gained awareness of Shiva. Such individuals also possess certainty about the Shiva principle. Their deep conviction about the power and sanctity of Shiva is strong as a rock.

Indeed we may extend this to all people of deep faith. They are not perturbed by arguments and propaganda against their profound faith in God. Likewise, those who have experienced the Divine at the highest level can also bring comfort to people. This is the role of the religious leaders in traditions. At the spiritual level, we all need to seek and find the experience, each in one's own way. But when people are in personal anguish, in emotional pain and confusion, the religiously enlightened can give comfort and solace: that is precisely what the poet says here about the Divine.

17.3

ஊற்றான உண்ணார் அமுதே உடையானே

ūṭṟāna uṇṇār amudē uḍaiyānē

Oh precious fount of ambrosia Who has me

Word Meanings

ūṭṟāna - as a spring, fountain

uṇṇār - precious

amudē - oh ambrosia

uḍaiyānē - of One who has (me)!

Explanatory Reflections

This line is connected to the previous one through the latter's last two words. Thus, it is *en chindaiyil ūṭṟāna*: that which is a fountain in my thoughts. The thought of the Divine is like a perennial spring in the poet's mind. The idea is that peaceful thoughts about the Divine are flowing spontaneously like waters from a fountain.

Those thoughts that flow in our poet's mind, he tells us, are like a divine potion: immortalizing ambrosia. It is a drink that is not easy to get, says the poet. It is a precious gift. Let it be noted that water from a spring is a natural outpour. Once again, the poet expresses the feeling that these thoughts for the Divine spring forth spontaneously in his mind. That

Divine mystical poetry offers us a taste of ecstasy which is what immortality is all about. Immortality in the physical body is not never-dying permanence but a short-lived experience of mystical ecstasy.

We may recall a similar metaphor from the Henry Wadsworth Longfellow's *Hymn to the Night* where we read:

From the cool cisterns of the midnight air
My spirit drank repose;
The fountain of perpetual peace flows there, -
From those deep cisterns flow.

17.4

வேற்று விகார விடக்கு உடம்பின் உள்கிடப்ப

vēṯṟu vigāra viḍakku uḍambin uḷkiḍappa

The different evils lying within the flesh of the body

Word Meanings

vēṯṟu - strange, different

vigāra - evil

viḍakku - flesh

uḍambin - of the body

uḷ - inside

kiḍappa - lying

Explanatory Reflections

There are two ways in which the human body is regarded in spiritualist traditions. One is to consider it sacred in as much as it is a temple where a spark of the Divine resides for a time.

The other is to regard it as impure and unclean, because associated with it are elements that are not conducive to spiritual growth. This line is a reference to the latter aspect. The body is an instrument for pleasure and pain. The pleasure is never pure. Sooner or later it leads to pain. Moreover, the pleasures that the body give are impermanent. Eventually they become beyond reach of the body, and then the body craves for it, leading to unhappiness.

The pleasures of the body create attachment,, and attachment is the cause of rebirth. The body's role as an impediment to spiritual growth is expressed in the New Testament (Matthew: 26.41) as: "Watch and pray that you may not enter into temptation. The spirit indeed is willing, but the flesh is weak."

In the spiritual framework there are eight kinds of evil (*vigáranggal*: These are: *kāmam*: desire; *ulōgam*: worldliness; *mōkam*: lust; *madam*: intoxication; *māṟchariyam*: jealousy; *iḍumbai*: arrogance; *poṟāmai*: envy. So when the poet says speaks of the flesh that is encased in the body, he is referring to all the evils that are associated with the human condition.

According to one school of early Christian writers (the *Patristics*), the eight evils corrupting human beings are: gluttony, lust. avarice, anger, sadness, restlessness, vainglory, and pride.

We recall a verse attributed to Sir Walter Raleigh (*The Lie Poem*):

Tell, zeal, it lacks devotion;
Tell love, it is but lust;
Tell time, it is but motion;
Tell flesh, it is but dust.

17.5

ஆற்றேன் எம் ஐயா அரனே ஓ என்று என்று

ātṟēn em aiyā aranē ō enḍṟu enḍṟu

I can't endure. Saying again and again, Oh Lord, Oh Siva

Word Meanings

ātṟēn - I cannot bear

em - my

aiyā - oh Superior One!

aranē - oh Shiva!

ō enḍṟu - saying that

enḍṟu - saying that

Explanatory Reflections

This line is a continuation of the previous one. It says in effect that the poet cannot endure any more this physical body with flesh and bones. He is appealing to the Lord that human birth has no more interest for him, for in his *sivañānam*, he has realized the inanity of worldly existence and its appeals.

This again is the heart-felt expression of a *bhakta* who has no more interest in or longings for the petty and transient things that delude the vast majority of people. So he pleads with God in terms that only true *bhaktas* can use.

In this line, the poet addresses God as *aiyā*. This is an important word in Tamil. It is the vocative form (form of address) of the word *aiyan,* which means an elder person, one for whom the addresser has great respect, even reverence. It could also mean father, teacher, or simply, Sir.

Sometimes the word is used to denote the deity *aiyanār* who, in the mythopoesie of the tradition, is an offspring of Shiva and Vishṇu.

The name *Aiyar* now refers to a Tamil Brahmin caste. It could also mean a man of wisdom. It does not have a feminine form. But in the caste classification of the Tamil world, Aiyar is a sub-caste whose members are Shaiva Brahmins. Generally Aiyars have no problem entering Vaishṅava temples, but Vaishṇavas avoided Shaiva temples, or so it used to be.

The word *aran* refers to Shiva. It is the Tamil version of the Sanskrit *Haran*. One name for Shiva's consort Pārvati is *araniḍattavaḷ*: She who is close to *aran*.

We may note that the revulsion of the physical body comes from the recognition that it is capable of many evil and unhealthy things. This is so not only in the Hindu tradition but also elsewhere. Thus, for example, we read in the New Testament (Galatians

5:16-21): "For the desires of the flesh are against the Spirit, and the desires of the Spirit are against the flesh, for these are opposed to each other, to keep you from doing the things you want to do. .... Now the works of the flesh are evident: lust, impurity, sensuality, idolatry, sorcery, enmity, strife, jealousy, fits of anger, rivalries, dissensions, divisions, envy, drunkenness, orgies and things like these."

It is not surprising that when one considers the body in these terms, one is really fed up with it, and wants to relinquish it to become one with the Cosmic Whole.

18.1

போற்றிப் புகழ்ந்திருந்து பொய்கெட்டு மெய் ஆனார்

pōṯṟi pugazndirundu poi keṭṭu mei ānār

Worshiped, lauded, untruth gone, truth became

Word Meanings

pōṯṟi - worshiped

pugazndirundu - being lauded

poikeṭṭu - untruth gone

mei - truth

ānār - became

Explanatory Reflections

The first word of this line is connected to the last words of the previous line, and must read *aiyā aranē endru endru pōtri,* which is to say: Oh Lord, oh Shiva, I have worshiped and lauded you again and again. And now, at long lost, I have been shorn of untruth, and have come to the Truth.

What is meant is that as a result of persistent worship and constant praising of the Lord, the poet has been transformed. He has been cleansed of all the falsehoods that clouded his mind, and he has at last seen the radiance that Truth is. This is a valid and effective mode of experiencing mystical merger: to worship the Divine in submission, and repeat the epithet of God's multi-splendors again and again, until at last all of God's glory gets so deeply etched that naught else is Truth anymore. Whether it is one of the various *sahasranamas* in the Hindu tradition, the rosary prayer of the Christian, or the *japji* of the Sikh, the repetition of God's name is implicit in many religious practices.

In this line, the poet also refers to an important principle in the psychology of learning. When we think we are learning something, actually we are also unlearning something else at the same time. We come to many subjects that we wish to learn, not only with ignorance, but also with pre-conceived misconceptions about the matter. So, in the process, our older views and understandings slowly melt away. Unless untruth is exiled, truth cannot enter the mind.

More specifically, by this line the poet may also be referring to other theologies which have an impact on one's mind. Indeed, in any religious context, we are faced with competing doctrines to which one might have succumbed or to which one is drawn. So when one is fully grounded in one's faith, one suddenly realizes that the doubts that troubled one's mind, as also one's inclinations towards other belief systems, were all merely hollow, for now at last one is in the full light of one's own Truth.

The full merger into the vision of one's tradition is the religious condition of the true believer in all denominational faith-systems. Once we have been transformed to a particular spiritual worldview, all else will seem meaningless and false. This is both the strength and the weakness of complete devotion to a deity, cult, religion, or system of philosophy (secular, political, or religious). Its strength lies in the steadfastness of the faith and the consequent spiritual fulfillment one experiences. The weakness is in its potential for intolerance and the devaluing of other faith traditions and belief-systems. Only a few enlightened souls are immune to this weakness.

18.2

மீட்டு இங்கு வந்து வினைப்பிறவி சாராமே

mīṭṭu iṅgu vandu vinaippiṟavi chārāmē

Coming again, may not my actions adhere

Word Meanings

mīṭṭu(m) - again

iṅgu - here

vandu - coming

vinai - action

piṟavi - birth

chārāmē - may it not adhere

Explanatory Reflections

We see in this line the reference to the *karma* doctrine again: Every consequential action results in rebirth. As noted before, this is a powerful framework in the Hindu framework. It not only explains the apparent injustices in the world, but is also a reason for renunciation, asceticism, and the like. By exerting to sever all detachments, one eradicates all cravings, for it is expected that one will have to come back (be re-born) in order to fulfill any wish which may be one's due as a result of good deeds.

The poet expresses his dislike for re-visiting the earth. Human birth will cause consequential actions, leading to another birth. We note here an important aspect of the *karma* framework, seldom stated explicitly. Though it is a law to which we are all subject, there is a mode of escaping it: By genuine devotion and heart-felt prayer. The idea is that appealing to the Supreme principle with the most genuine supplications, it is possible to be relieved of the never-ending chain. Indeed, this is one of the unstated reasons for daily prayer. For in chanting the prayer the devotee is directing the thoughts to the Divine, and by this means one rids oneself of some of the re-birth generating loads that we all accumulate in the course of our lives.

In this sense, one may be relieved from the cycle by God's mercy. In Shakespearean words, mercy "droppeth as the gentle rain from heaven upon the place beneath." We are also reminded of the lines of William Wordsworth (*Memorials of a Tour in Scotland*):

Sweet Mercy! to the gates of Heaven
This Minstrel lead, his sins forgiven;
The rueful conflict, the heart riven
With vain endeavour,
And memory of Earth's bitter leaven,
Effaced for ever.

18.3

கள்ளப் புலக்குரம்பைக் கட்டு அழிக்க வல்லானே

kaḷḷap pulakkurumbaik kaṭṭu azikka vallānē

Bind and destroy this deceiving sensory body

Word Meanings

kaḷḷa - stealthy

pula - sensory

kurambai - body

kaṭṭu - bind

azikka - destroy!

vallānē - oh mighty one!

Explanatory Reflections

The body with its senses is deceitful, says the poet. This is not only a statement of philosophical significance, but also of scientific validity. The senses enable us to experience many things, but only in distorted ways. Much of what our senses create is really not there in the physical world. There is neither color nor smell nor taste nor sound, but only waves and particles which are perceived as different sensations by the body. Our sensory faculties map an experiential reality that has a correspondence with physical reality. But most often we mistakenly identify this experienced reality with the external physical reality. We are reminded here of Immanuel Kant's distinction between the noumenon and the phenomenon.

There are also illusions created by our senses. There seems to be nothing between us and the clouds, but there is, in fact, the invisible atmosphere consisting of vast amounts of oxygen and hydrogen and other gases. The sun seems to rise and set, which it really does not. The moon seems to wax and wane, but it really does not. We can go on and on. Albert Einstein put it succinctly: "Reality is merely an illusion, although a very persistent one."

The body deceives us in two other ways: By making us think that all the pleasures we experience are ever-lasting. The impermanence of worldly enjoyments is what makes them not real at all, for reality, for the spiritual aspirant, never decays or dies. Moreover, by drawing us to all the petty pleasures, they also sow the seeds for re-birth. So we are bound by the ropes of physical experiences for which we crave because of our sensory faculties. Having realized all this, the poet feels that he has had enough of this terrestrial experience.

This is the reason for praying for the bondage to be cut off and to never again be reborn. As Arthur Schopenhauer's reflected (*Parerga and Paralipomena*):

VARADARAJA V. RAMAN

How very paltry and limited the normal human intellect is, and how little lucidity there is in the human consciousness, may be judged from the fact that, despite the ephemeral brevity of human life, the uncertainty of our existence and the countless enigmas which press upon us from all sides, everyone does not continually and ceaselessly philosophize, but that only the rarest of exceptions do.

18.4

நள் இருளில் நட்டம் பயின்று ஆடும் நாதனே

naḷ ḷ iravil naṭṭam payinḍr̲u āḍum nādanē

Oh Lord, who is in a (cosmic) dance at midnight

Word Meanings

naḷ - middle

iruḷ il – in darkness

naṭṭam - dance

payinḍr̲u - occurring

āḍum - dancing

nādanē - oh Lord!

Explanatory Reflections

The poet's reference to midnight reminds one of the comment by Antoine St. Exupéry (*Flight of Arras*): "Night, when words fade and things come alive. When the destructive analysis of day is done, and all that is truly important becomes whole and sound again. When man reassembles his fragmentary self and grows with the calm of a tree."

In this line we find an explicit reference to the magnificent Naṭarāja of holy Chidambaram. In simple English, Naṭarāja means king of dance, the Dancing Divine. But this phrase hardly conveys the spiritual power and esoteric significance of this most important symbol in the Hindu world.

In Hindu spiritual framework the Shiva principle is engaged in the cosmic dance at the moment of dissolution of one eon and the creation of the next. Hence the dance at midnight which is the boundary point between two days. Creation and dissolution are dynamic processes, involving action and energy, and there are cosmic vibrations when they occur. There is also universal joy when the universe ceases, only to be born again. That is the significance of the dance which is rhythmic energy.

The physical world is sustained by countless elementary particles at the sub-nuclear level. These come and go, i.e. they are incessantly created and annihilated in accordance with certain fundamental principles. The Dance of Siva is sometimes interpreted as reflecting those basic episodes in the microcosm that are invisible to us, but which have been revealed to be at the root of physical reality.

So when the poet invokes Naṭarāja, he is essentially expressing his recognition of the deep-down Reality that keeps this universe functioning. For there can be no world, no universe, no matter and no energy without the unseen and unfathomable principle that is at the core of it all. In the course of our daily chores, we rarely even think of the deeper truths about being and becoming. It is the recognition of that ultimate core through spiritual and poetic visions that constitutes spiritual realization.

As Ananda Coomaraswami wrote in his *The Dance of Shiva,* Nataraja is

the clearest image of the activity of God which any art or religion can boast of… A more fluid and energetic representation of a moving figure than the dancing figure of Shiva can scarcely be found anywhere.

15.5

தில்லை உள் கூத்தனே தென்பாண்டி நாட்டானே

tillai uḷ kūttane ten pāṇḍi nāṭṭānē

Oh Dancer in Tillai of the Pāṇḍiya realm

Word Meanings

tillaiyuḷ - in Tillai

kūttane - dancer

ten - south

pāṇḍi - Pāṇdiya

nāṭṭānē - Oh One of the Country/Kingdom

Explanatory Reflections

A little familiarity with geography and history is necessary for understanding this line. First, *Tillai* is another name for the pilgrimage town which is also known as Chidambaram. The town is known by other names too, such as *Kōyil* and *Puṇḍarīkapuram*. It is here that the famed Temple of Nataraja is located. This temple is regarded as one of the most sacred shrines in the Tamil world. Here is the famous *Chitsabha* where, as per sacred history, the Cosmic Dance of Naṭarāja actually occurred. In this temple may be found sculptures of various canonical poses of the *Bharata Nāṭṭiyam*, the traditional dance of Tamil India, as well as icons of the sixty three *Nāyanmārs* who are the pillars of the Tamil Shaiva framework.

In pure Tamil, *kūttu* simply means dance. Thus *kūttan* is a dancer. This is an epithet for Lord Shiva.

The PāṇDiyā kingdom was one of the three major kingdoms that covered the Tamil land in distant times, the Chēra and the Chōza being the other two. It was ancient enough to have been known to Megasthenes and Ashoka before the Common Era, and to Pliny and Ptolemy in the first century of the Common Era. Archeologists have unearthed Roman coins there, showing that there had been trade with Rome. At one time, the three kingdoms were attacked by a certain Achchuda Kaḷappan. When this happened, the kings of these three kingdoms are said to have met in *Ten Tillai,* Southern Tillai or Chidambaram. The Pāṇḍiyā kings gained full control in the sixth century CE.

That Naṭarāja is associated with Tillai is the reason the poet refers to Shiva as of the Southern Tillai country. This is like referring to Christ as Jesus of Nazareth, with this difference that whereas Christ is a historical figure geographically located, Shiva is a cosmic transcendental figure belonging to sacred history.

More importantly, this line is a reference to the

fact that the poet received his inspiration and mystical experience in this part of the world. It is somewhat like referring to Our Lady of Fatima or of Lourdes because in those places there had been visions of Mary.

19.1

அல்லல் பிறவி அறுப்பானே ஓ

allal pi̱ravi a̱ruppānē ō

The Supreme One who cuts off evil birth

Word Meanings

allal - evil

pi̱ravi - birth

a̱ruppānē - Who cuts off

ō - Superior One

Explanatory Reflections

Again and again, we see the poet revert to this basic theme: That the Shiva principle cuts off the chain of birth and death. Indeed, as explained in the introduction, this is a central tenet of Saiva Sidhāntam: the *pāsam* or rope that is binding the *pasu* (creatures) is cut off by *pati* the Siva principle.

What this means is that Divine grace can release us from the cycle of birth and death. This leads to merger with Brahman which is equivalent to what, in some other religious frameworks, is described as going to heaven. The metaphor of a rope as a binding force that chains us to the world of ephemeral reality is interesting. When an animal is tied to a rope it can move here and there around the pole to which it is tied, but never break away from the confinement. Within the confines it feels as if it is free. Likewise, when we are in the cycle of birth and rebirth we feel as if we are free in the course of our lives. When the rope is cut, the creature is set free. This is equally true in the case of the enchained soul.

In a way we may draw a parallel between this and the Christian notion of Christ being the Savior. The Savior is one who redeems us from all our sins, and when we are thus redeemed, we become eligible for the celestial abode. We read in the Book of Job: "I know that my redeemer liveth." For ultimately what matters is the freedom one gets when the constraints of being human are removed.

The point is, with all its charms and pleasures, terrestrial life is not the ideal state for the human soul, for two reasons: First it is always associated with pain and suffering. Second, in its embodied state it does not fully understand, appreciate, or experience the ecstasy that comes from merger with the Cosmic Whole.

This eagerness to end life may sound too pessimistic. But if we hold the belief that a release would take us to infinite bliss, then it is not pessimistic but positively optimistic, for there is the conviction that all the sufferings concomitant with physical life will cease to be, and that we will be trading in the petty pleasures (*chiṯrinbam*) of terrestrial existence for something far more significant and precious. It is like the difference between a child accustomed to its toys and the maturer state of an adult whose experience of life is at a much higher level.

Another way of looking at the notion of Shiva as being the reliever of the birth-death cycle is by invoking Shiva's role as a member of the *trimūrti:* which is to dissolve the universe after the completion of a *kalpa*: a full Brāhmic day which lasts for more than eight billion years. The *saṃsāra* cycle is ended by that act of Shiva's Cosmic conflagration also.

19.2

என்று சொல்லற்கு அரியானைச் சொல்லித் திருவடிக்கீழ்

enḍṟu chollaṟku ariyānaich chollit tiruvaḍikkīz

One whom words can't speak of, under His holy feet

Word Meanings

enḍṟu - thus, that

chollirku - for saying

ariyānai - the difficult one

cholli - saying

tiru - sacred

(v)aḍi - feet

kīz - beneath

Explanatory Reflections

Mystics have compared their experience to sweetness and fragrance that cannot be adequately described in words.

Donkeys that can only bray
Can't know the joys of those who pray,

Even great poets have recognized the inadequacy of words for conveying the deepest feelings and experiences. Alfred Lord Tennyson wrote (*In Memoriam*):

My words are only words, and moved

Upon the topmost froth of thought.

It is not surprising that when one tries to describe God in words, that tends to be rather ineffective. John Milton put it this way *Paradise Lost* VII.8.5):

To resound almighty works
What words or tongue of seraph can suffice?

That is why many great mystics and visionaries have often declared that the spiritual experience is ineffable.

And yet, that is precisely what great poets and visionary try to do. They make every effort to put in words their most profound intuitions about the Divine. We may ask, Why do they do that? It is for the benefit of those who have not had such experiences. By their writings the seers and saints are conveying to the rest of us an inkling of what they themselves have experienced. Like photographs taken by a traveling member of the family, they share it with the rest of us. The pictures are never more than a fraction of what the traveler experiences, but at least they give the non-traveler some idea of what it was all about. Having done that, the poet, in the gesture of a true *bhakta*, falls prostrate at the feet of the Divine.

As noted earlier, respect and reverence to gods

and elders are shown by touching their feet. Hence the Divine is sometimes involved in terms of the holy feet. We may recall the words of St. Therese of Lisieux: "What a joy it was for me to throw flowers beneath the feet of God!"

19.3

சொல்லிய பாட்டின் பொருள் உணர்ந்து சொல்லுவார்

cholliya pāṭṭin poruḷ uṇarndu cholluvār

Who understand and recite the uttered hymns

Word Meanings

cholliya - the said (recited)

pāṭṭin - of the song (verse)

poruḷ - meaning, inner essence

uṇarndu - understanding

cholluvār - they say (recite)

Explanatory Reflection

The hymns of a tradition may be approached from different perspectives:

The first way is to listen to them when they are properly chanted with the appropriate rhythms. In this day and age, thanks to audio technologies, we are able to do this in many ways. In earlier times, we had to be in the presence of trained gurus for this. The second way is to recite them oneself with deep devotion. Neither of these modes calls for an understanding, superficial or deep, of what is being recited. As one swamiji said in a lecture,

Monks living in the forests of the Himalayas chant *aum* or sing something else and play upon a musical instrument. Many times snakes, deer, and wild beasts of the forests leave their places and come up to the side of the monks. Now, these wild animals understand nothing of the laws of music, nothing of the chanting of *aum,* still the effect is there. If the mere sound produces such a marvelous effect upon snakes and deer, cannot the mere sound chanted continually in the right time produce an effect in your life?

In fact, it is through such sonic repetitions that religious traditions have been maintained during countless generations. Repetitions by the devout, more than its exposition by scholars, is what makes the sacred works of traditions last for a long time. If two generations of children are not introduced to the traditional framework, that will be the demise of the entire tradition.

However, the inner meanings of the verses chanted are seldom clear to the average follower of a tradition. Even their literal meanings are not always easy to understand when they are expressed in sophisticated language, and that too with ancient words and allusions. In order to derive full benefit from such works we need people who not only understand the abstruse passages, but also see through their inner meanings. They sometimes interpret the chants to the lay people in their own ways. These are the people who preserve the meaning and message of the works over the centuries. Sometimes, by giving additional meanings, they also enrich the tradition.

We note that the poet says *uṇarndu cholluvār*. The first word here means not just understanding, but understanding with feeling: an important concept in the religious context. The poet is suggesting that the reciter of spiritual poetry should not only understand what is recited in its literal and deeper meanings, but should also fully internalize and realize what it is all about. When it is chanted thus, it carries much more weight than when somethingis uttered through rote learning.

Then there is another way of approaching these works: That is in the framework of scholarship. Here the exponent of the wisdom and the reader may not necessarily be a spiritual aspirant. When one delves into the work as a detached student, one regards it as the expression of a mystic genius whose work is a precious legacy of humanity's culture. Such a scholar has no fervor or commitment to any particular sect or school of thought. For such a one, whatever is best in the human spirit deserves respect and reverence, from no matter which culture or tradition it emanates.

19.4

சலெ்வர் சிவபூரத்தின் உள்ளார் சிவன் அடிக்கீழ்

chelvar sivapurattinn uḷḷār sivanaḍikkīz

The fortunate ones in Shiva's realm who are under his feet

Word Meanings

chelvar - happy/fortunate persons

siva - (of) Shiva

pur̲ attin - in the city

uḷḷār - insiders

sivan - Lord Shiva

aḍi - feet

kīz - underneath

Explanatory Reflections

In the previous line the poet mentioned people who fully understand and recite the hymns of Shiva. Here he says that such people will come to reside in the Sivapuram or the realm of Shiva. There are two ways of interpreting this line: A literal interpretation could be that such souls will eventually attain, to use the phrase of another tradition, the Kingdom of God. Indeed, such a heaven, in the words of Shakespeare, is "the treasury of everlasting joy." Or, as the nineteenth century poet James Montgomery

(*Friend After a Friend Departs*) put it,

There is a world above,
Where parting is unknown;
A whole eternity of love,
Form'd for the good alone;
And faith beholds the dying here
Translated to that glorious sphere.

Another interpretation of our poet's line could be that those who fully internalize the significance of this hymnal wisdom will discover an inner peace that is more rewarding and fulfilling than any other satisfaction.

To say that in such a state they will be under the feet of the Divine simple means that they will be governed by Divine visions and values, by the knowledge that all people are children of the same Divinity. In this recognition, they will feel love and compassion towards all fellow beings. This is because our mental and spiritual wellbeing is largely a function of what we think and feel deep in our mind and heart.

Irrespective of the kinds of heaven that may be there in the unknown beyond, there is a heaven well within our reach during our sojourn on earth. The *Sivapurāṇam,* like all other sacred works of humanity, is a route by which we may experience a little of that earthly heaven, besides ensuring a passage to another heaven elsewhere at another phase of our continuance in the cosmos.

Note that the poet refers to those people as the fortunate ones. This is because in his framework it is through Divine grace that one arrives at it. He draws this conclusion from his own personal experience. He did not do penance or go in search of God, but he came upon the revelation almost by chance. He received grace. Indeed, each and every one of us has received any number of gifts in life, large or small, without our asking. All our in-born positive qualities and capabilities are of this kind. They may therefore appropriately be called grace.

19.5

பல்லோரும் ஏத்தப் பணிந்து

pallōrum ēttap paṇindu

Many, laud him in reverential bow.

Word Meanings

pallōrum - many people

ētta - lauding

paṇindu - bowing in reverence

Explanatory Reflections

The work ends appropriately with a praising reverential bow, for that is what worship of God ultimately is. Worship is not only the recognition, but also the recalling of God's greatness from the sacred history of the tradition, and the extolling of God's glory. A hymn, says a dictionary, is "a song of praise, adoration, thanksgiving, etc., especially one sung at a religious service." In this sense the Sivapurāṇam is a hymn. For it is also sung in temples in religious services. In keeping with the observation of George Herbert's criterion (*A True Hymn*):

The fineness which a hymn of psalm affords
Is when the soul unto the lines accords

the Sivapurāṇam is truly a hymn, or, as one would say in Tamil, this is a *pāsuram*.

However, there is more than praise, poetry, and

piety in this work. The saint has revealed to us many aspects of the Shiva principle, he has recalled for us the worldview of Saiva Siddhāntam, and he has shown us how *Siva bhakti* can express itself through the voice of a poet.

The worshiper is not content with silent meditation. Except in its highest state, and for ordinary people silent meditation on the abstract does not result in the kind of ecstasy that heart-felt chanting of God's names and attributes provides. There is no limit to those attributes, offering the worshiper unlimited opportunities for explicitly mentioning them. But it is the poet and the devotional saint who articulate these in ways by which we simple folk can recite and repeat them. Without composers, inspired poets, and mystics, there would be no hymns or chants, no *shlokas* and *stotras* to be recited at home or in temple or church in any tradition.

If we sing God's glories, we should do so with humility. Humility comes from the recognition, not simply of one's own finiteness, but also of the possible virtues and greatness of others compared to oneself. Nowhere does it become more appropriate than in the presence of the Almighty. There is no room for those who imagine themselves to be high and mighty to be anywhere near that which is already High and Mighty.

The concluding line reminds us that the many who reverentially bow to the Divine will attain many spiritual benefits. Herein lies the value of chanting religious verses.

Here end my reflections on Sivapurāṇam.

MANIKKAVASAKAR'S SIVAPURANAM

Sivapurāṇam
Tamil Text
Transliteration
Meaning

1

நமச்சிவாய வாழ்க 1நாதன் தாள் வாழ்க
இமைப்பொழுதும் என் நெஞ்சில் நீங்காதான் தாள் வாழ்க
கோகழி ஆண்ட குருமணிதன் தாள் வாழ்க
ஆகமம் ஆகிநின்று அண்ணிப்பான் தாள் வாழ்க
ஏகன் அநேகன் இறைவன் அடிவாழ்க

namachchivāya vāzga nādaan tāl vāzga!
imaippozudum enneñjil nīṅgādān tāḷ vāzga!
kōkazi āṇḍān kurumaṇi-tan tāḷvāzga!
āgamam āgi-niḍṟu aṇṇippān tāḷ vāzga!
ēgan anēgan iṟaivan aḍi vāzga!

May Siva's name endure! May the feet of the Lord (who guides me) endure!
Who will not move away from my heart even for a moment, may He endure!
May the feet of the spotless gem of Kōkazi endure for ever!
May the feet of the One Who became the Agamas endure for ever!
May the feet of the One-Many God endure!

2

வேகம் கெடுத்தாண்ட வேந்தன் அடி வெல்க
பிறப்பறுக்கும் பிஞ்ஞகன்தன் பெய்கழல்கள்
வெல்க
புறந்தார்க்குச் சேயோன் தன் பூங்கழல்கள் வெல்க
கரங்குவிவார் உள்மகிழும் கோன்கழல்கள் வெல்க
சிரம்குவிவார் ஓங்குவிக்கும் சீரோன் கழல்
வெல்க

vēgam keḍuttāṇḍa vēndan aḍi velga
pi̲rappa̲rukkum piññagantan peikazalkal velga
pu̲rattārkkuch chēyōn tan pūṅkazalkaḷ velga
karaṅkuvivār uḷmagizum kōnkazalgaḷ velga
chiram kuvivār ōṅguvikkum chīrōn kazal vega

May the feet of the lord who arrested the speed be victorious!
Who cuts the cycle of rebirths, may his boon-giving feet be victorious!
May the flowered feet of Him who is far from unbelievers be victorious!
The kingly feet of Him whose worship gives inner joy, may they be victorious!
May the feet of the One who raises those that bow with their head be victorious!

3

ஈசன் அடிபோற்றி எந்தை அடிபோற்றி
தேசன் அடிபோற்றி சிவன் சேவடி போற்றி
நேயத்தே நின்ற நிமலன் அடி போற்றி
மாயப் பிறப்பு அறுக்கும் மன்னன் அடி போற்றி
சீரார் பெருந்துறை நம் தேவன் அடி போற்றி

īsan aḍipōṭṟi endai aḍipōṭṟi
dēsan aḍipōṭṟi sivan chēvaḍipōṭṟi
nēyattē ninḍṟa nimalan aḍi pōṭṟi
māyap piṟappu aṟukkum mannan aḍipōṭṟi
cīrār perunduṟai namdēvanaḍi pōṭṟi

Praise be unto Siva's feet, praise be unto my Father's feet!
Praise be unto the Effulgent One's feet, praise be unto Shiva's red feet!
Praise be unto the feet of the Pure One who stands for all that is good!
Praise be unto the feet of Him Who cuts the illusive birth!
Praise to the feet of the splendid one of Perunduṟai!

4.

ஆராத இன்பம் அருளும் மலை போற்றி
சிவன் அவன் என்சிந்தையுள் நின்ற
அதனால்
அவன் அருளாலே அவன் தாள் வணங்கி
சிந்தை மகிழச் சிவ புராணம் தன்னை
முந்தை வினைமுழுதும் ஓய
உரைப்பன் யான்

sivan avan en chindaiyuḷ nindṟa adanāl
ārāda inbam aruḷum malai pōṯṟi
avan aruḷālē avan tāḷ vaṇaṅgi
chindai magiza sivapurāṇam tannai
mundai vinai muzudum ōya uraippan yān

Praise be unto the Mountain that bestows the
grace of non-satiating joy!
Because he, Sivan, remains in my mind.
By His grace, having paid homage to His feet
The mind-delighting Sivapurāṇam
To erase the effects of all past I will chant.

5

கண் நுதலான் தன்கருணைக் கண்காட்ட
வந்து எய்தி
எண்ணுதற்கு எட்டா எழில்ஆர் கழல்
இறைஞ்சி
விண் நிறைந்தும் மண் நிறைந்தும்
மிக்காய், விளங்கு ஒளியாய்
எண் இறந்த எல்லை இலாதானே நின்
பெரும்சீர்
பொல்லா வினையேன் புகழுமாறு
ஒன்று அறியேனே

kaṇṇudalān tan karuṇai kaṇkāṭṭavandu eidi
eṇṇudaṟku eṭṭā ezilār kazal iṟaiñji
viṇ niṟaindum maṇ niṟaindu mikkāi, viḷangu
oḷiyāi
eṇ iṟanda ellai ilādānē nin peruñchīr
pollā vinaiyēn pugazumāṟu ondraṟiyēn

The Three-eyed One having come to with His
merciful glance,
Bowing reverentially to the feet of the
unreachable beautiful One

Filling air and land and shining grandly:
O fully great One beyond the limits of thought
As one of evil deeds, I do not know how to laud (the Lord). 25

6

புல்லாகிப் பூடாய்ப் புழுவாய் மரமாகி
பல் விருகமாகிப் பறவையாய்ப் பாம்பாகி
கல்லாய் மனிதராய்ப் பேயாய்க்
கணங்களாய்
வல் அசுரர் ஆகி முனிவராய்த்
தேவராய்ச்
செல்லாஅ நின்ற இத் தாவர
சங்கமத்துள்

pullāgi pūḍāi puzuvāi maramāgi
pal virukamāgi pa̠ravaiyāi pāmbāgi
kallāi manidarāi pēyāi kaṇaṅgalāi
vallasurarāgi munivarāi dēvarāi
cellā a ninḍ̠ra ittāvara chaṅgamattuḷ

After becoming grass, shrub, worm, and tree;

After being a prairie dog, bird, and snake;
After being stones, humans, mean spirits, and petty beings;
After becoming powerful asuras, sages, divine beings;
In all moving or unmoving living things which stood, in that stable union.

7

எல்லாப் பிறப்பும் பிறந்து இளைத்தனே்,
எம்பரெுமான்
மயெ்யே உன் பரொன் அடிகள் கண்டு
இன்று வீடு உற்றனே்
உய்ய என் உள்ளத்துள் ஓங்காரமாய்
நின்ற
மயெ்யா விமலா விடைப்பாகா
வதேங்கள்
ஐயா எனவோங்கி ஆழ்ந்து அகன்ற
நுண்ணியனே

ellāp pi̱rappum pi̱randiḷaittēn emperumān
meyyē un pon aḍigaḷ kaṇḍu inḍṟu vīḍu uṭṟēn

uyya en uḷḷattuḷ ōṅkāramāi ninḍṟa
meiyyā vimalā viḍaippāgā vēdaṅggaḷ
aiyā ena ōṅgi āzndu aganḍṟa nuṇṇiyanē

I became tired of taking all births, my Lord.
In truth, seeing your golden feet, I have achieved emancipation today
That I may benefit, standing in my heart as the Om-syllable.
As truth, as purity, as the Bull, the Vedas
Elevated, as O Lord (by the Vedas), deep, all-pervasive, O subtle one! 35.

8

வெய்யாய், தணியாய், இயமானனாம் விமலா
பொய் ஆயின எல்லாம் போய் அகல வந்தருளி
மெய் ஞானம் ஆகி மிளிர்கின்ற மெய்ச் சுடரே
எஞ்ஞானம் இல்லாதேன் இன்பப் பெருமானே

அஞ்ஞானம் தன்னை அகல்விக்கும் நல்
அறிவே

veiyyāi taṇiyāi iyamānanām vimalā
poi āyina ellām pōi agala vandaruḷi
mei ñānamāgi miḷirgiṇḍṟa meich chuḍarē
eññānam illādēn inbapperumānē
aññānan tannai agalvikkum nal aṟivē

As harsh and mitigating, as Master, the
blemishless One,
All untruth removed by grace that came,
O brilliant one that is magnificent as true
(I am) without an iota of wisdom, O loving
Lord!
O benign wisdom that removes ignorance! 40

9

ஆக்கம் அளவு இறுதி இல்லாய்,
அனைத்து உலகும்
ஆக்குவாய் காப்பாய் அழிப்பாய் அருள்
தருவாய்

போக்குவாய் என்னைப் புகுவிப்பாய்
நின் தொழும்பின்
நாற்றத்தின் நேரியாய், சேயாய்,
நணியானே
மாற்றம் மனம் கழிய நின்ற
மறையோனே

ākkam aḷavu iṟudi illāi anaittulagum
ākkuvāi kāppāi azippāi aruḷ taruvāi
pōkkuvāi ennai puguvippāi nin tozumbin
nāṯṟattin nēriyāi cēyāi naṇiyānē
māṯṟam manam kaziya ninḍṟa maṟaiyōnē

You are without transformation, measure. The
whole world
You create, protect, destroy, and give grace.
You have sent me here to make me part of those
who serve you.
Subtler than fragrance, Who is far and near!
You, Who is in wisdom, transcending word and
mind 45

10

கறந்த பால் கன்னலொடு நெய்கலந்தாற்
போல
சிறந்தடியார் சிந்தனையுள் தேனூறி
நின்று
பிறந்த பிறப்பு அறுக்கும் எங்கள்
பெருமான்
நிறங்கள் ஓர் ஐந்து உடையாய்,
விண்ணோர்கள் ஏத்த
மறைந்திருந்தாய், எம்பெருமான்

karanda pāl kannaloḍu nei kalandāṟ pōla
chiṟandaḍiyār chindanaiyuḷ tēn ūṟi ninḍṟu
piṟanda piṟappu aṟukkum eṅgaḷ peṟumān
niṟaṅgaḷ ōr aindhu uḍaiyāy, viṇṇōrgal ētta
maṟaindirundāi enperumān

As fresh milk is like sugar-candy and ghee
In the minds of great devotees You stood as flowing honey
Our Lord Who cuts off the (future) births of the born ones
United in the five colors, lauded by celestials.

You were hidden, O my Lord! 50

11

வல்வினையேன் தன்னை மறைந்திட
மூடிய மாய இருளை
அறம்பாவம் என்னும் அரும் கயிற்றால்
கட்டி
புறம்தோல் போர்த்து எங்கும் புழு
அழுக்கு மூடி
மலம் சோரும் ஒன்பது வாயில்
குடிலை
மலங்கப் புலன் ஐந்தும்
வஞ்சனையைச் செய்ய

valvinaiyēṉ tannai maṟaindiḍa mūḍiya māya
iruḷai
aṟam pāvam ennum arum kayiṭṟāl kaṭṭi
puṟam tōl pārttu eṅgum puzu azukku mūḍi
malam chōrum onpadu vāyil kuḍilai
malaṅgap pulan aindum vañchanai cheiyya

Out of potent evil deeds one's true self closed,

the darkness of illusion
Bound with the rare rope of sin and merit,
Seeing the outer skin, the filth and worms being covered
Impurity flows through the nine doors of the hut
The sensory faculties confuse and deceive. 55

12

விலங்கு மனத்தால், விமலா உனக்கு
கலந்த அன்பாகிக் கசிந்து உள் உருகும்
நலம் தான் இலாத சிறியறேர்க்கு நல்கி
நிலம் தன்மலேல் வந்து அருளி
நீள்கழல்கள் காட்டி
நாயிற் கடையாய்க் கிடந்த அடியறேர்க்கு

vilaṅgu manattāl vimalā unakku
kalanda anbāgik kasindu uḷ urugum
nalam tān ilāda chiṟiyēṟku nalgi
nilamtanmēl vandu aruḷ i nīḷ kazalgaḷ kāṭṭi
nāyiṟ kaḍaiyāi kiḍanda aḍiyēṟku

With enchained mind, to you, O unblemished one
Mingled with love, the tender heart melts.
Showing grace to petty ones who are without any good
Coming to earth, you blessed us and showed your majestic feet
To the slave who lay being inferior to a dog 60

13

தாயிற் சிறந்த தயா ஆன தத்தூவனே
மாசற்ற சோதி மலர்ந்த மலர்ச்சூடரே
தசேனே தனே் ஆர்அமூதே சிவபூரானே
பாசமாம் பற்றூ அறூத்தூப் பாரிக்கூம் ஆரியனே
நசே அரூள்பூரிந்தூ நெஞ்சில் வஞ்சம் கடெ

tāyiṟ chiṟanda dayā āna tattuvanē
māchaṭṟa chōdi malarnda malarchuḍarē
tēsanē tēnār amudē siva purānē
pāsamām paṭṟu aṟuttup pārikkum āriyanē

nēsa aruḷ purindu en neñjil vañcham keḍa

O Lord of Nature, more magnificent in
compassion than mother!
O spotless, splendid, blossomed flowery
brilliance!
O illustrious one, O honeyed ambrosian, O
dweller in Sivapuram!
O Master, who severs the chain of bondage and
appears!
From your friendly grace my illusions are
dispelled.   65

14

பரோது நின்ற பரெுங்கருணைப்
பரோராறே
ஆரா அமுதே அளவிலாப் பமெ்மானே
ஓராதார் உள்ளத்து ஒளிக்கும்
ஒளியானே
நீராய் உருக்கி என் ஆருயிராய்
நின்றானே
இன்பமும் துன்பமும் இல்லானே

உள்ளானே

pērādu ninḍṟa paruṅkaruṇaip pōrāṟē
ārā amudē aḷavilāp pemmānē
ōrādār uḷḷ attuḷ oḷikkum oḷiyānē
nīrāi urukki en āruyirāi ninḍṟānē
inbamum tunbamum illānē uḷḷānē

O all-embracing river of mercy who envelops
Never-satiating immeasurable great God!
O Luminous One that shines in the hearts of
even those
who know not!
O, He stood, as the fullness of my soul was
fluidly molten,
The One who is with and without joys and
sorrows!

15

அன்பருக்கு அன்பனே யாவையுமாய்
இல்லையுமாய்
சோதியனே துன்னிருளே தோன்றாப்
பெருமையனே

ஆதியனே அந்தம் நடுவாகி அல்லானே
ஈர்த்து என்னை ஆட்கொண்ட எந்தை
பெருமானே
கூர்த்த மெய் ஞானத்தால் கொண்டு
உணர்வார் தம்கருத்தில்

anbarukku anbanē yāvaiyumāi illaiyumāmāi
chōdiyanē tunniruḷē tōnḍṟāp perumaiyanē
ādiyanē antam naḍuvāgi allānē
īrttu ennai ātkoṇḍa endai perumānē
kūrtta mei ñānattāl koṇḍuṇarvār tam karuttil

Friend of friends, all and nothing too,
O radiant one, O great one near whom no
darkness comes!
O Origin of all, one without middle and end!
O great Lord who drew and accepted me!
Through keen wisdom will they know its
significance. 75

16

நோக்கரிய நோக்கே நுணுக்கரிய நுண்

உணர்வே
போக்கும் வரவும் புணர்வும் இலாப்
புண்ணியனே
காக்கும் என் காவலனே காண்பரிய பேர்
ஒளியே
ஆற்றின்ப வெள்ளமே அத்தா மிக்காய்
நின்ற
தோற்றச் சுடர் ஒளியாய்ச் சொல்லாத
நுண் உணர்வாய்

nōkkariya nōkkē nuṇukkariya nuṇ uṇarvē
pōkkum varavum puṇarvum illāppuṇṇiyanē
kākkum en kāvalanē kāṇpariya pēr oḷiyē
āṯrinba veḷḷamē attā mikkāi ninḏṟa
tōṯṟach chuḍar oḷiyāi chollāda nuṇ uṇarvāi

Who is difficult to focus on, and subtle to grasp,
O Holy One without entry or exit or links!
O my guarding warden, effulgence too bright to behold!
O flooding river of ecstasy, O Father Who stands in splendor!

Who appears as brilliant light, You grasp the most subtle unuttered things.

17

மாற்றமாம் வையகத்தின் வெவ்வேறே
வந்து அறிவாம்
தேற்றனே தேற்றத் தெளிவே என்
சிந்தனை உள்
ஊற்றான உண்ணார் அமுதே
உடையானே
வேற்று விகார விடக்கு உடம்பின்
உள்கிடப்ப
ஆற்றேன் எம் ஐயா அரனே ஓ என்று
என்று

māṯṟamām vaiyagattin vevvēṟē vandu aṟivām
tēṯṟanē tēṯṟat teḷivē en chindaiyuḷ
ūṯṟāna uṇṇār amudē uḍaiyānē
vēṯṟu vigāra viḍakku uḍambin uḷkiḍappa
āṯṟēn em aiyā aranē ō enḍṟu enḍṟu

As various changes in the world, and as

knowledge too,
O Truthful One (Who brings) clarity to mind!
O precious fount of ambrosia Who has me!
The different evils lying within the flesh of the body
I can't endure, saying again and again, O Lord, O Siva 85

18

போற்றிப் புகழ்ந்திருந்து பொய்கெட்டு மெய் ஆனார்
மீட்டு இங்கு வந்து வினைப்பிறவி சாராமே
கள்ளப் புலக்குரம்பைக் கட்டு அழிக்க வல்லானே
நள் இருளில் நட்டம் பயின்று ஆடும் நாதனே
தில்லை உள் கூத்தனே தென்பாண்டி நாட்டானே

pōṭṟi pugazndirundu poi keṭṭu mei ānār
mīṭṭu iṅgu vandu vinaippiṟavi chārāmē

kaḷḷap pulakkurumbaik kaṭṭu azikka vallānē
naḷ ḷ iravil naṭṭam payinḍṟu āḍum nādanē
tillai uḷ kūttane ten pāṇḍi nāṭṭānē

Worshiped, lauded, untruth gone, truth
became,
Coming again, may not my actions adhere!
Bind and destroy this deceiving sensory body,
O Lord, who is in a (cosmic) dance at midnight!
Oh Dancer in Tillai of the Pāṇḍiya realm!

19

அல்லல் பிறவி அறுப்பானே ஓ
என்று சொல்லற்கு அரியானைச்
சொல்லித் திருவடிக்கீழ்
சொல்லிய பாட்டின் பொருள் உணர்ந்து
சொல்லுவார்
செல்வர் சிவபுரத்தின் உள்ளார் சிவன்
அடிக்கீழ்
பல்லோரும் ஏத்தப் பணிந்து

allal piṟavi aṟuppānē ō

endṟu chollaṟku ariyānaich chollit tiruvaḍikkīz
cholliya pāṭṭin poruḷ uṇarndu cholluvār
chelvar sivapurattinn uḷḷār sivanaḍikkīz
pallōrum ēttap paṇindu.

The Supreme One who cuts off evil birth;
One whom words can't speak of, under His holy feet;
Those who understand and recite the uttered hymns,
The fortunate ones in Shiva's realm who are under his feet,
Many, laud him in reverential bow.

Select Bibliography

Aiyangar, S. Krishnaswami *Some Contributions Of South India To Indian Culture* The University of Calcutta Press, 1923.

Arulsamy, S., *Saivism – A Perspective of Grace,* New Delhi. Sterling Publishers Private Limited, 1987.

Flood, Gavin, *An Introduction to Hinduism,* (Ch. 7) Cambridge UP, 1996.

http://www.saivaworld.org (For information on World Saiva Council).

Nair, Kunhi, *Sages Through Ages* – Volume V: India's Heritage, IN: Bloomington, Author House, 2007.

Pillai, JM Nallaswami, *Studies is Saivasiddhanta,* Charleston, SC, Nabu Press, 2010.

Raman, V. V., *Indic Visions in an Age of Science,* New York, NY: Metanexus, 2011.

Raman, V. V. *Voyage through Indic Heritage,* Cr.Sp, NC

Schomerus, H. W. and Palmer, H., (Translation Mary Law), *Saiva Siddhanta: An Indian School of Mystical Thought (Presented as a system and documented from the original Tamil Sources),* New Delhi, Motilal Banarsidass, 2002.

Printed in Great Britain
by Amazon

59641713R00189